WINNING POINTS WITH THE WOMAN IN YOUR LIFE

ONE TOUCHDOWN AT A TIME

JACI RAE

A Fireside Book
Published by Simon & Schuster
New York   London   Toronto   Sydney

FIRESIDE
Rockefeller Center
1230 Avenue of the Americas
New York, NY 10020

WINNING POINTS WITH THE WOMAN IN YOUR LIFE
ONE TOUCHDOWN AT A TIME™ is a trademark owned by
North Shore Records and Jaci Rae.

First Fireside Edition 2005

FIRESIDE and colophon are registered trademarks
of Simon & Schuster, Inc.

For information regarding special discounts for bulk purchases,
please contact Simon & Schuster Special Sales at 1-800-456-6798
or business@simonandschuster.com.

Manufactured in the United States of America

10 9 8 7 6 5 4 3 2 1

ISBN-13: 978-0-7432-9419-5
ISBN-10:   0-7432-9419-X

All football terms used in this book are listed in Chapter 20
to assist you with their meaning if you are unfamiliar with them.

CONTENTS

FOREWORD . . . . *v*

CHAPTER 1   Stepping into the Stadium 1

CHAPTER 2   Getting onto the Field—Shedding a Little Light on the Complex
World of Male-Female Relationships: Why We Are the Way We Are 5

CHAPTER 3   Avoiding the Defensive Lineman and the Backfield 11

CHAPTER 4   Learning to Avoid Incomplete Passes—Communication 17

CHAPTER 5   Learning to Key—Women Feel Their Words, Hear Them 23

CHAPTER 6   Hitch and Go Doesn't Work in Relationships—Do What
You Say, Say What You Do 31

CHAPTER 7   The Huddle—Emotional Word Pictures 37

CHAPTER 8   Getting Benched—The Difference Between a Man's "No"
and a Woman's "No" 41

CHAPTER 9   Making the First Round Draft Pick with Romance 45

CHAPTER 10   Learning the Playbook: The Memory Game 57

CHAPTER 11   The Team—True Intimacy, the Road to Becoming Better Friends 63

CHAPTER 12   Recruiting and Stats—Things Women Need You to Know 75

CHAPTER 13   The Chemistry of Love—Scientific Facts 89

CHAPTER 14   Illegal Procedures—Women in the Wallet, Women in the Frames 93

CHAPTER 15   Adding Value to Your Team—Spending and Investing Time 101

CHAPTER 16   Looking for a Draw Play—Nonverbal Communication 107

CHAPTER 17   The Last Pass—How and Where to Meet the Woman or Man in Your Life
If You Don't Currently Have Anyone to Score a Touchdown With 111

CHAPTER 18   Getting into the End Zone Consistently—The Final Word 119

CHAPTER 19   Relationship Advice from Legendary NFL Clutch-Kickers 123

CHAPTER 20   Football Definitions, Rules, Penalties and Fun Football Stats 143

CHAPTER 21   Epilogue 159

Foreword

"Men and women belong to different species, and communication between them is a science still in its infancy." - *Bill Cosby*

When Jaci Rae first contacted me regarding her new book, *Winning Points with the Woman in Your Life, One Touchdown at a Time;* I was intrigued and maybe a little skeptical. Could THIS book actually entice men to pick it up and hold their attention as it describes differences between the sexes and provides advice on how to better understand, connect and communicate with their partner?

As I verbalized some of my initial thoughts to Jaci, I said something like, "If the subject doesn't relate to sports, news or politics, it usually won't appeal to many guys." At this point, Jaci began to read aloud from the table of contents and I found myself thinking, "brilliant."

Jaci Rae took what she knows about men, which is a lot, and wrote a book that speaks directly to them, in a language they know and understand very well. Her creative use of football metaphors to explain how women think, feel and behave has made this book not only very informative, but also easy and FUN to read. Her writing covers a whole range of critical components needed for successful relationship building, including; understanding how men and women are different, the real definition of chemistry, active vs. passive listening, common pitfalls in intimate communication, listening vs. hearing, differences in the way men and women express themselves, and how to connect with a woman through building real friendship and intimacy- to name a few.

Even though I am not a true football fan, I found it difficult to put this book down. Each chapter presents an important nugget of information and offers clear and rational supporting facts and descriptive vignettes all wrapped in a sports themed package. On almost every page, the reader can find an interesting football fact that keeps them hooked and turning the pages for more. I thought of all the women who could benefit from this book as well, because it offers great insights into how men are wired and the influence this has on their view of the world and their (at times confusing) behavior.

When I read the chapter on how men and women use language differently because of cultural and biological differences; I found myself thinking of the many couples I have worked with who had reached an impasse in their communication due to their inability to sit down together to share feelings and resolve issues to their mutual satisfaction. In these sessions, I often found that the woman had read more into something her partner had said because, as Jaci points out so well, "women have a natural intuition that drives them to dig deeper and search for hidden meaning."

On the other hand, the man's perspective was usually that he had said what he had to say- with no hidden meanings or agendas attached. In this kind of all too common scenario, the woman usually feels he is holding back and not sharing himself with her and the man feels that she is looking for something negative because she is angry with him for not agreeing with her point of view and/or giving in. As Jaci talks about this, she uses the metaphor of a football "play". This is when each "player must learn a specific language that tells them how to respond to their teammates on the field." When every player understands the techniques and how they are executed - it unites them into a winning team. Now this is something a guy can relate to.

In my counseling and coaching work, I have often heard one partner express anger at the other because they are hearing one thing but experiencing another from them. Jaci addresses this with her "Hitch and Go" play. This is when, for instance, "a player fakes a turn to catch a pass and then continues downfield for a deeper one."

Every football fan knows and loves this one. However, Jaci points out that this will not work in a relationship. She calls the play beautifully when she says we need to, "Do what we say and say what we do, or anger and hostility will result from the promises made but not kept." The next time a woman raises this issue in coaching, I plan to turn to her male partner and talk about the danger of using a "Hitch and Go" play. I'm pretty sure I will save some valuable session time and not have to worry about his eyes glazing over as I try to find a way to relate her feelings to something that he can understand.

One of my favorite parts of this book is when Jaci talks about building friendship and true intimacy. Her descriptions of how men and women differ in the ways they seek and attain intimacy are perfectly articulated. Men are visual and tactile and seek physical contact with women they find physically desirable. Women, on the other hand, crave emotional intimacy. They want to know how the man thinks and feels, what he believes, and what is important to him. If not understood, these differences can lead to her belief that he is more interested in sex than in her, and his belief that she controls him with sex because she has little desire for it.

Neither of these is true; but when they are believed, they lead to the kinds of issues that many couples come into counseling for. Along with identifying and explaining this difference, Jaci offers great advice to men on how to achieve emotional intimacy. Her suggestions are concrete and easy for guys to implement. She emphasizes the important point that for women- intimacy is really all about the little thoughtful things that a man does, or does not do in the relationship.

One of the most important things Jaci says in this chapter is that, "Just as a football team will look for a player to replace you if you aren't fulfilling your role, a woman will draft another player into your position if you aren't meeting her basic needs in the relationship." Too many men figure this out too late in the game.

Even though this book speaks in the language of football, it will have great appeal to women as well. Here they will find a list of traits that men say can be found in an "almost perfect female." They will also get a man's perspective on the "Don't Go There Ever" woman. Want a list of the top five things men say you should know about them? This book has it. Want to know what to say and do to keep him happy or perhaps get a view into his thoughts when you say, "let's talk?" My personal favorite is the list of "top five things that women do that make you crazy or get on your nerves." Fasten your seatbelts ladies- this is a great ride.

Jaci also offers many ideas and suggestions on ways to spend quality time together, how and where to meet the woman or man of your dreams and how to help your relationship thrive. Again, she gives concrete and practical tips that are sure to offer something to every reader. This is a book I would highly recommend to every man and woman who is interested in improving and/or deepening his or her intimate relationship. Speaking to the guys out there, I would say that finally there is a book on relationships that won't leave you feeling like you've been dragged to another "chick flick." To the ladies I would say, "read this and you will never again have to ask, why do guys act like that." In addition, he will be impressed by your incredible knowledge of football."

—Toni Coleman, LCSW

Toni Coleman, MSW is a licensed psychotherapist and relationship coach with over 20 years of experience helping singles and couples achieve their relationship goals. As a recognized expert, Toni has been quoted in many local and national publications and has been featured on *abcnews.com; discovery.health.com; aolnews.com; MSN.com*, and *Match.com*. As a weekly contributing commentator (love and dating coach) on the *KTRS Radio Morning Show*, (St. Louis, MO); she offers dating tips and relationship advice. Toni is also the featured relationship coach in the newly released book, *"The Business And Practice Of Coaching*, (September 2005)."

Toni is the author of many popular articles on meeting, dating, communicating, single life and healing from relationship loss. These can be found on over thirty dating and singles oriented web sites and in several lifestyle magazines. She founded *Consum-mate.com* in 2002 to offer singles the knowledge and tools they need to find and sustain healthy, lasting love relationships. Her monthly newsletter, The Art Of Intimacy, helps thousands of subscribers with its dating and relationship advice. Toni is also the featured relationship coach in the newly published book, *The Business and Practice of Coaching*. Toni is a member of The International Coach Federation, The International Association Of Coaches and The National Association of Social Workers.

CHAPTER 1
Stepping into the Stadium

As you step into the stadium for the first time, your entire body and mind are filled with both anticipation and apprehension for what lies ahead of you in the coming season. As the new star quarterback, a great many things will rest upon your shoulders.

Chief among them: How many yards will your team gain on the very first down of your very first game? You see, you want it known upfront that you are a team to be reckoned with. Will you run or pass the ball? Will you call an audible or use the coach's plan? How will you ultimately win the most games, with as few fumbles, penalties and pass interferences as possible, so that you can eventually make it to the Super Bowl?

Obviously, no one steps into the stadium to lose. But, what do you need to actually win? This time-honored question remains on the lips and deep in the minds of every coach and player today.

And yet, thousands of books, countless practices and a seemingly endless number of games, both won and lost, have gone into generating the wisdom and foresight attained by the most talented coaches and players, those who can best answer this question. They have come to understand that the answer boils down to the responses learned from reading, watching and practicing. The same set of guidelines applies to relationships, where men and women of all ages ask the exact same question: "How do I win in the game of love?" Of course, the answer doesn't change either. In order to win, you need to learn and practice the rules of engagement.

This book is meant to be a guideline for some of those rules. I am sure that if you are reading this book, you are already interested in learning. The next step will be to practice, practice, practice! The way to learn to play solid football is to get on the field, but that can happen only after you have read the playbook and carefully listened

Fun Football Fact: In what year and in which stadium was the first NFL playoff game ever played?

to valuable advice from experienced coaches and players. The team and the coach will test you on the playbook once you have entered onto the field.

To learn about women, you have to do exactly the same thing as the players do on a football team. You can't get onto their field and into their end zone simply by guessing. You have to prepare first, learning all that you can about that playing field you are about to enter onto and the team you are about to join. If you want to win at love, you will need to gain the same trust, honor, and respect from the woman in your life that the players on your team have for you.

Fun Football Fact:
The first NFL playoff game was held indoors at the Chicago Stadium in 1932.

While mistakes happen in any game -- and relationship-- many can be prevented by learning the right set of moves and using the correct language, that will get you off the bench, in the game and eventually into the end zone. Anything worth having is worth working for and the right relationship is definitely worth that work. Any successful player knows that firsthand. They know that you have to read the playbook, review the action, listen carefully, and sweat a lot!

Just as Tom Dempsey (November 8, 1970) and Jason Elam (October 25, 1998) both kicked 63-yard record - breaking field goals, you too will make a record-setting kick in your relationship if you treat the woman in your life with honor and respect. Treat her like a queen and she'll treat you like you were Tom Brady or Jerry Rice! So grab a towel and a jug of Gatorade, put on your shoulder pads, helmet, uniform and cleats. Let's head out onto the field and learn why men and women are so different and what a woman needs to satisfy her man.

Even if that statement sounds confusing now, it will become clearer as you continue to read. One of the most valuable lessons you can learn is that once your mate is satisfied, you will be in for the game of your life as she will want to show her appreciation and satisfy you! Above all, women want men to understand them, just as men want to be understood by women. There is nothing new about that concept. All living beings want to be treated with loving care, kindness and concern.

Therefore, the amount of loving care, kindness and concern that you bestow on a woman will directly affect the way she treats you. So sit back, relax, and enjoy making it to the Super Bowl of relationships and winning! Now let's step onto the playing field. *"There should be no division in the body, but that its parts should have equal concern for each other." 1 Corinthians 12:25*

Oops! I almost forgot to give you your pep talk before you stepped out of the locker room, so here goes. This book will give you a brief look into the world and mind of a woman, including the way she thinks and how to score points with her, while suffering the least number of penalties or turnovers.

It should be noted that the material in this book pertains to a majority of the general population of men and women. Of course, there are exceptions -- those men who are more "right-brain" oriented and those women who lean towards the "left-brain."

Additionally, in writing this book, I am not implying that the responsibility of the entire relationship rests solely on the shoulders of the man. Rather, this book is only one tool, a tool designed to help men better understand women in order to enhance their relationships. Even though this book is written to help men comprehend more factually why women are the way they are, it is actually a book that will help both sexes learn to understand and better communicate with each other. You can apply these facts, values and thoughts to any relationship in your life.

Since I am a woman, I am better qualified to write about how women think, feel and act. Through my experiences, I have come to learn what I want and need from a man in order for me to react favorably to him.

The conclusions that I have come to in this book are a result of a lifetime of these experiences as well as years of reading about, being a part of, and watching both successful and unsuccessful relationships unfold. Any additional insight I have gained, is the zenith of the countless years I have spent studying about and interviewing people involved in both successful and unsuccessful relationships. For this book in particular, I have also interviewed men and women of various ages and backgrounds to gather a deeper understanding into their needs, wants and desires. This book is the culmination of all those interviews, along with my own personal experiences and the facts that I have gathered throughout my life's journey.

It should be stated that the type of men or women that you initially attract into your life will be based upon your own personal belief system about yourself and the world around you.

This book will be a very useful tool as you work to create a winning relationship no matter what your personal values are either consciously or subconsciously. So with that said, let's walk into the stadium and onto the field of love.

Fun Football Fact:
Who came up with the name Super Bowl?

CHAPTER 2
Getting onto the Field
Shedding a Little Light on the
Complex World of Male-Female Relationships:
Why We Are the Way We Are.

So you've made it into the stadium and you are now stepping onto the playing field for your first day of practice with the Dallas Cowboys. Nervous excitement courses through your veins as the coach talks about the various formations he is going to run the team through and begins to discuss the different play calls and strategies he will be using during this season's games.

While much of what the coach talks about initially lies within the realm of football common sense and comes easily to you, there are a few nuances in the game plan that you will be unfamiliar with. Also, some of the plays are new to you and could cause complications and confusion in the season ahead if you don't understand them. A team's language will guide you in how to interact and communicate with your teammates on the playing field. This language that each player must learn is full of individual components, called the "plays." For each "play," there is a "plan." Each of these "plays" and "plans" has been specially formulated through years of research and scientific study, producing entire systems of proven techniques that can make winners out of the players and teams.

Once the methods were proven effective, they were gathered together and worked into a playbook for each team to base its "plays" and "plans" on. It is that playbook that each teammate must learn in order to be part of the winning team. This process is much the same as that of the "plays" and "plans" of a relationship. You need to read the manual, learn from those who are already where you want to be in their relationships and listen actively to your

Fun Football Fact:
The term "Super Bowl" was created by Lamar Hunt, owner of the Kansas City Chiefs.

partner in order to learn how to speak their language. Once you learn this language, you can enter the game confidently and achieve victory!

A woman's perception of her relationship, as well as the language she uses within a relationship may seem very complicated, and sometimes confusing. You may find particular things in her language syntax that are hard to understand and certainly difficult to interpret! And as if that weren't enough, many women have a tendency to turn over and over in their heads most of what is said to them, finding more than what may actually be there.

While men tend to go with the flow without over-analyzing things, women try to find out what's behind the words they see and hear when dealing with their loved ones. This process is intuitively part of their naturally protective circuitry, helping them emotionally guard themselves and their loved ones. Have you ever heard the statement, "You don't want to mess with Mother Bear?" This applies here because women are built as nurturers and maintain a natural curiosity about their environment, in order to help them protect themselves and those they love from perceived dangers.

This natural curiosity triggers what I like to call the "need to know" gene. Women have the "need to know" or to discover all the "information" about their surroundings and then make judgment calls as to any dangers that may affect those they love. This of course, can lead to any number of natural responses to the perceived dangers of their surroundings and an inherent desire to analyze all causes and effects. Because curiosity (analyzing) is a natural response for women, it tends to bleed over into other areas of their lives, namely their relationships.

In addition to analyzing most of what is said to them, women may often have hidden meaning in what they say, even if they don't intend to put it there. Men are not as complicated (in a good way) with their spoken language. What men say is most often what they mean. So, why is it that so many women seem to include hidden messages behind their words? In the same way that women tend to over-analyze things, sometimes they also include hidden meaning in their spoken words. The reasons for this can be partially found by looking at the traditional upbringing and social history of women. Parents and other adults teach women, at a very early age, that they need to be strong, confident and know what they want. They are also told that they need to be assertive and independent in order to succeed at fulfilling their dreams and desires for their future.

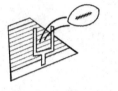

Fun Football Fact:
Which coach has won the most games in NFL history?

In reality, though, oftentimes the media image of a woman is much different. Society in general, sees images of successful women on television and in the movies that are more demure and non-aggressive, but still get what they need and desire.

The woman on television or in the media, who ends up with the man of her dreams, may have played it "coy," playing off on her seeming "need" for the man. The media image presented is often in direct conflict with the way that a woman may have been raised. Because of these two conflicting images, women have now received mixed messages and are subjected to confusing images about the way they should behave in society. On top of this, women see the men around them as being intrigued and often fascinated by the media image of a woman, an image that may not always interconnect with the ideals and values that they, as women, were brought up with.

Because of this, women may be unsure how to present themselves and may seek to bring forward aspects of both images at the same time. As a result, they may confuse the two images, hiding their true feelings and thoughts deep within their words, all the while struggling to achieve the final goal of communicating their needs or "message" to those that participate in their lives.

A perfect example of a woman who was portrayed in this fashion by the media was Princess Diana. Because she was portrayed as being meek, mild mannered, demure, and fragile, both men and women were fascinated and intrigued with her. Not only was she a beautiful princess, but she also seemed emotionally vulnerable, as well a woman a man could take care of; for many men, she was a fantasy of the "perfect" woman.

Fun Football Fact: Don Shula has won the most games in NFL history. He won his 325th game on November 14, 1993 as the coach for the Miami Dolphins. On that date, the Dolphins defeated the Philadelphia Eagles 19 - 14.

In reality, though, Princess Diana was a fiercely independent woman, a tigress capable of fighting when it came to what she believed in, someone who went after what she wanted with a tireless passion. This truth, and the truth of many women beyond Princess Diana, differs greatly from the images often times portrayed in the media. Are you beginning to understand the playing field a little bit more? Great, then let's move on to…

Chemistry and Environment

Our environment has a great deal to do with how we relate and react to each other as well as how we communicate with other people. Another huge factor in our character make-up is the individual chemistry that everyone is born with. While much has been said about how different the sexes are, how much do we actually know? The facts show that men and women are conceived equally in terms of their overall intelligence.

However, somewhere between the twelfth and fourteenth weeks of pregnancy, there is a testosterone wash that flows over the brain of a male baby. [i] This wash does not take place during the formation of a female baby. Let's take a look at how the brain works and try to understand why this is so important.

Testosterone is one of the main chemicals that enable the brain to manufacture and create serotonin, which is an important neurotransmitter in the brain, causing certain nerve cells in the brain to activate and become livelier. Serotonin can also act as an inhibitor. Most neurotransmitters can act as both an exciter and an inhibitor. Serotonin affects the brain's interior, known as the ganglia.

The ganglia are the network of the brain, which is divided into two cells, the L cell and the R cell. Scientists believe that one of these cells makes serotonin and the other produces dopamine. Dopamine is "a monoamine neurotransmitter formed in the brain and is essential to the normal functioning of the central nervous system. [ii]" Dopamine acts as an inhibitor in the ganglia, thereby causing a calming effect and dampening activity.

It is believed that during the testosterone wash, a balance between the L cells and the R cells are set, determining the amount of serotonin and dopamine that the brain's network will use. This also determines how spatially or temporally aware a person is, with men being born more spatially aware and women more temporally aware. A person who is spatially aware is generally a "left-brain" individual and someone who is temporally aware, is generally a "right-brain" individual.

The word "spatial" is defined as "relating to space. [iii]" As men are generally more spatially aware, they tend to be better at judging distances, which comes in handy during parallel parking! The word "temporal," meanwhile, is defined as being "of or limited by time. [iv]" This may explain why women seem to be able to associate time and events without much difficulty. You know what I am talking about here men, that little thing that really bothers men about women -- she remembers everything she thinks you have done wrong and when you did it! I believe this is due in part because of a woman's propensity for temporal awareness.

Because of the testosterone wash, men tend to be more "left- brain" oriented and women rely more readily on the "right-brain." "Left-brain" individuals tend to be more interested in facts, inclined to logic and reason. They are more motivated in providing

Fun Football Fact:
What do C.C. Pyle, the NFL and AFL all have in common?

for the home and usually more interested in becoming engineers, mathematicians and scientist. These are just a few career choices that a "left-brain" individual might make.

A "right-brain" individual tends to be better at, and more interested in, developing relationships and dealing with emotional issues. They are more inclined to emotions and passions and are generally more motivated by investing in the relationships of the home. Their career choices tend to put them in the roles of care-givers or into jobs where they can use their artistic, investigative and research abilities.

This is in contrast to the general tendencies of "left-brained" individual. Again, a clearer picture begins to be revealed when we look at the differences between the sexes in this light. Most men might find a leisurely reading of *Popular Mechanics* or *Programmer's Security Desk Reference* fundamentally more interesting than reading *Ladies' Home Journal* or *Parent Child Magazine*, while women are just the opposite. This is simply a matter of one's interest and NOT an intellectual issue, as both men and women can be motivated for various reasons to read on all the subjects mentioned. Remember that both sexes are born equally in terms of intelligence.

An interesting bit of trivia: The top women's magazines, as reported by the *US Market Research Report*, are those dealing with lifestyle, fashion and homemaking. They include *Better Homes and Gardens, Family Circle, Good Housekeeping, Woman's Day, Ladies' Home Journal, O Magazine, Redbook, Cosmopolitan, Vogue* and *Glamour*. The top men's magazines? *Playboy* (Now there's a shocker! More on this later.), *PC World, Sports Illustrated, Newsweek, Business Review Weekly* and *Golf Digest*.

Back to our look at individuality and what makes us all so unique and special. A "left-brain" individual (generally a man) wants to conquer, while a "right-brain" individual (generally a woman) wants to give sympathy and look for sequence. There's the basic chemistry lesson for now.

Here is an observation that I made of a man who wanted to conquer and a woman who was looking for sequence. There was a man and a woman who were mountain biking on a very steep and rocky road. When they reached the top of one of the steepest grades on the road and were facing an equally steep drop, the woman didn't seem to be enjoying the ride as much as the man.

With a pained expression on her face, she seemed to be saying, "How am I going to get down this mountain without getting hurt or breaking my bike?" Her eyes darted back and forth as she

Fun Football Fact:
In 1926, C.C. Pyle petitioned the NFL for a franchise. When they refused, he started the first AFL (American Football League), which held nine teams, including the Grange's New York Yankees and the Philadelphia Quakers.

The AFL lasted only one year and folded shortly after the New York Giants shut out the Philadelphia Quakers 31 - 0 in December of 1926.

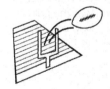

Fun Football Fact:
What historic event took place for the Baltimore Ravens on January 28th, 2001?

analyzed the drop. While she was carefully trying to find the best sequence of maneuvers that would keep her safe while getting her down the hill, the smile on the face of the man said it all. His eyes gleamed and seemed to say, "Yeah! Cool hill! I'm going straight down, really fast! I'm the man!" While he was elated, she was not. Men are geared for speed and love to conquer and that's exactly what he was going to do.

My uncle gave me a funny example the other day of how men see women's thought patterns when it comes to making decisions. I thought that this insight was a great example of men conquering and women looking for sequence and order before they tackle the matter at hand.

Here's what he had to say: "Men rule by action. Women rule by committee. For example: Man sees hill, climbs hill. Woman sees hill, forms discussion group, sets up hill climbing committee, votes for hill climbing team, schedules climb date, checks rain fall charts, does studies to locate best path, sends out scouts, and much, much, much, much later...finally climbs the hill."

The Good News

The facts stated thus far pertain only to our pre-disposition at birth. The things we experience each day, the lessons that we are taught as we move through our daily lives and the personal choices we make along the way will also be determining factors in how "left-brain" or "right-brain" we become. These factors will also directly affect our communication with and relationship to others.

The good news is that since each of us has the freedom to make personal choices, we can learn to hear and understand each other's language when we step onto the playing field to begin practice! *"Your hands made me and formed me; give me understanding to learn your commands." Psalms 119:73*

Once you step up and onto the playing field, however, you will need to hear exactly what the coach has to say during practice if you want to make it to your first game. So listen up!

CHAPTER 3
Avoiding the Defensive Lineman
and the Backfield

As you probably already know, the defensive lineman's job is to sack the quarterback. As the quarterback, if you want to sidestep the defensive lineman and "scramble" in your relationship, you will need to learn the difference between actively hearing and passively listening to the woman, i.e., "the defensive lineman" in your life.

Just as the head coach for the Miami Dolphins needs his team to hear what he has to say about certain plays and plans in order to communicate the winning strategy, so does your partner. If a team member doesn't listen enough to the coach during the practices, he may end up on the bench for the first game. Being benched for too many games and he becomes a liability to the team and runs the risk of eventually being cut from the roster entirely.

There is a very important distinction between actively hearing and passively listening. Later on, I will share with you how women feel their words. This should give further insight into the reasons why "hearing" is so important to women. For now, however, let me give a brief explanation as to why I choose to make a firm distinction between these two phrases. In your lifetime, I'm sure you've heard over and over the frustrated expression, "Do you hear what I am saying?!" Why do you think the word "hear" is used instead of "listen?" To find out, let's look at the actual difference between these two words.

While the meaning of the word "listen" is "to make an effort to hear something, [v]" "hear" means "to learn by listening" or "to listen to attentively. [vi]" Can you see the real distinction between these two words? To "listen" implies the action of simply "making an effort" to hear something, whereas the word "hear" implies the action of "learning" through that action. It's a personal choice as to whether we "listen to" (make an effort) or "hear" (learn) what is

Fun Football Fact:
On November 12, 1953, Judge Allan K. Grim of the U.S. District Court in Philadelphia upheld the NFL policy of blacking out home games.

being said to us. I believe the phrase "selective hearing" applies to listening, implying the act of actually putting up barriers to learning, while the phrase "active hearing" applies to the process of truly learning about what someone has to say.

The man in my life actively hears everything I say. It always amazes me when he listens to me recount the details of my day or a particular event for an endless amount of time and then comments on things I have said throughout my long spell of talking. He is actually learning about who I am and what I cherish. How do I know he is actually learning?

Let me give you an example. Almost everyone who has gone to school has had the following experience. A huge test is coming up in a class that you need to study for. While you have listened in class, made notes, passed smaller tests and written papers on the subject matter at hand, you still are not well versed in it. Why? Because you haven't really learned the subject for whatever reason.

For the big test you cram the night before for all the information outlined to you during class so that the subject matter will be fresh for the next day's exam. The day of the exam you do really well and pass with flying colors.

Now let's jump ahead a few years. Someone asks you questions on that same topic, but you don't quite recall the information. While anyone can cram for a test the day before a final, not everyone can remember a few years later what they learned during their cram session. Why? Because they didn't really learn it. They simply stored the majority of the information in their short term memory banks. When someone actively hears what is said to them, they are learning the subject matter just as the man in my life learns about me, thereby storing or indexing the information he has learned about me in his long term memory banks.

So how do I know he is learning about me when I talk to him? Because he will bring up something I would consider a very minute and insignificant detail I shared with him either about my life or something that happened in a particular day quite a while later (meaning not even on the same day or perhaps even the same week or month). When he does this, he endears himself to me and causes me to feel special and honored in a way that no other man has ever done. I am always deeply moved when I have conversations with him and he remembers what I have said. This causes me to want to become even more dedicated to his needs and desires. So don't "cram" for your partners' information. Actively hear.

I have heard many women use the phrase "selective hearing" when it comes to the men in their lives. Why is that? It's because they perceive that the men in their lives are not hearing, and therefore not learning, about the way they feel or think or about what has happened to or around them during their day. If you want to get past the defensive backfield or any "red dogging" or "blitzing" that might occur, you need too avoid miscommunication and learn to hear what your partner is saying to you, no matter how trivial you think the topic currently on the table for discussion may be.

Men Are at the End Zone; Women Are at the Kick Off

On average, men speak between 12,000 to 13,000 words a day and women use between 25,000 and 26,000 words per day. [vii] This means, that by the time men have reached the two minute warning in the fourth quarter of the game and they need to make a touchdown to win, women are just getting warmed up!

So what are the implications of this? When a man is ready for the locker room after the end of the game, and a long cool swig of Gatorade - i.e. ready to go home and have dinner - a woman is just getting ready for the verbal kick-off when the man walks through the door! That means, when a man finishes a long day at work, he has probably reached his maximum daily quota of words spoken. By the time he arrives home, he may want nothing more than to eat dinner in peace and quiet and then curl up with a book or watch television on the sofa next to his loved one. Basically, he has finished with his fourth quarter and is now on his way off the field, completing his game day.

For a woman, on the other hand, even after a long day at work or time at home with the children, she may have only achieved half of her maximum daily quota of words spoken and is ready for the second half of the game, setting up a clash. After discovering this interesting fact, I could see why some men think that many women are chatterboxes!

And yet, although our differences seem to be daunting, they're also what make us such a unique and perfect match. We are each halves that together make a perfect whole. It was designed that way. *"Then the Lord God said, 'It is not good that the man should be alone; I will make him a helper fit for him.'" Genesis 2:18*

Fun Football Fact:
On January 26, 2003, which team won their first Super Bowl?

So how do we bridge the gap to better understand one another? Since our chemistry has already pre-determined so much of our individual identities, we have to learn how to speak each other's language. Here's where I wish there was a universal translator -- like the one they have on *Star Trek*.

A universal translator would allow every single species to speak the same language. Think about how much easier a path we would have if we could simply understand exactly what the other sex was really saying as they were saying it. For now, however, the words and the meaning behind them of the opposite sex may as well be a foreign language to our ears.

Fun Football Fact:
On January 26, 2003, the Tampa Bay Buccaneers won their first Super Bowl. They defeated the Oakland Raiders 48 - 21 in Super Bowl XXXVII at the Qualcomm Stadium in San Diego, CA.

Foreign Language 101

Have you ever felt that, when listening to someone of the opposite sex, you were listening to a foreign language that you had never heard before? Or wondered why it was that, when you said something to the opposite sex, they looked at you with a quizzical gaze? You don't understand why they didn't get it?

In the movie *Sleepless in Seattle*, there's a scene where Sam and Greg are talking about dating and a letter that Sam has received from a woman named Annie. Suzy (Greg's wife) tells them that it reminds her of the movie *An Affair to Remember* and goes into great detail about the movie and its plot. Sam and Greg look dumbly at her and then at each other with their eyebrows raised and their eyes rolling back, before declaring, "That's a chick flick!" They perceive that she is speaking a foreign language and do not understand why she is getting so worked up over a movie. With great concern, Sam's son Jonah (Jonah is seven years old) asks Suzy "Are you alright?"

Sam and Greg respond, "Yes," with a look of disgust on their faces. While she is telling them about the story with the right side of her brain, which wells up her emotions, they are thinking from the left side of the brain and wondering what the point of the whole story is and how it is relevant to their conversation.

Even more, they want to know when her emotional outbreak is going to end and begin to tease Suzy and talk about *The Dirty Dozen*, pretending to get worked up as much as she did. If you watch this portion of the movie, you will see a very clear and funny portrayal of male versus female language and thought processes. Recently, I overheard a couple locked in an argument, helping to give me better insight on a more personal level into the differences

Fun Football Fact:
What sport was first televised as game of the week?

between male and female language. The woman was crying with great emotion, "You're missing the point I'm trying to make!" I thought his reply was classic. He retorted back in a very matter-of-fact tone, "Well I wish you'd get to the point then!"

While she had thought that she was making her feelings clear in plain English and had already made "the point," he really had no idea what she was talking about and was getting more frustrated by the minute. He, as a "left-brain" individual, wanted to express and discover the facts, while she, as a "right-brain" individual, wanted to express her emotions and feelings. Does this sound familiar? Of course it does.

Here is another example of two people engaged in an interaction with common words that ended up having two totally different meanings attached to them. The wife of a friend of mine had made spaghetti as the main course for dinner. When the husband innocently said to her, "This is good tonight!" he quickly found himself wearing the spaghetti instead of eating it. "What went wrong?" he wondered. He had given her a compliment and she had inexplicably reacted with anger.

While they both spoke the same literal language, in this case English, they had reached different interpretations of the words used. When inquiring as to why she had reacted this way, she said that she thought he was saying to her that the spaghetti was good while every other night's food wasn't. This proves to be a case of words carrying a different weight because of the feelings attached the words or the perceived meaning behind them. Basically the indexing of the words in each person's personal dictionary or what I call, "word history."

Simply put, men and women have different feelings attached to the words they use in everyday life - their word histories. These word histories then make up a different style and type of dictionary for each individual. There will be more on word histories in later on. As stated before, although hormones initially induce differences between the male and female species, we can learn to hear and speak each other's language. Similarly, a defensive lineman who has been traded from the Green Bay Packers to the Philadelphia Eagles can learn the variances in his new team's "plays" and "plans."

However, he must carefully listen to the coach, read the playbook and watch the verbal and non-verbal language of the other players to better understand the differences between his language and that of his new teammates.

Fun Football Fact:
The NFL was the first sport televised as the game of the week. The event took place on October 3, 1948. The teams? It was the Brooklyn Lions against the Buffalo Bills, 21-31.

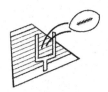

Fun Football Fact:
When were the points awarded for a field goal changed from five down to four?

Fun Football Fact:
In 1904, the points awarded for a field goal were changed from five to four.

Deciphering each others language is much the same. Even so, if you've already read this far, you're on the path to better understanding your mate's language and graduating from Foreign Language 101. Remember: you can do anything that you put your mind to! *"I can do everything through Him who gives me strength."* *Philippians 4:13*

CHAPTER 4
Learning to Avoid
Incomplete Passes—Communication

An incomplete pass can occur for several reasons, not the least of which is miscommunication. Communication is of the utmost importance in any game. If you are the quarterback of the Denver Broncos, and you are about to be sacked, your only option may be the "Hail Mary," throwing the ball into the air without a specific player in mind and hoping that someone on your side will catch it.

Since no prior communication has taken place, it's a very risky maneuver. If you let communication go in any relationship, you are running the same risk as the quarterback throwing a "Hail Mary." You are hoping that the partner on your team will catch the ball and run it for you.

The word "communication" means "the exchange of thoughts, messages, or information. viii" As stated earlier and shown by various examples, "right-brain" individuals have a tendency to interpret words, actions or the lack thereof, in ways that may not have originally been intended by the person who "passed the ball."

Let me give you another example that may sound very familiar to you. A friend of mine had been dating a man for a few months. During that time, he had always used the words, "I want to see you." After a few weeks of separation due to an extended business trip, he finally called her.

He said that he didn't have a lot of time to talk, but wanted to find out how she was. Even though he expressed that he was there for her and that he missed her, when they ended the phone conversation, he didn't set a date to see her again. His parting words were

Fun Football Fact:
How did the Chicago Bears get their name?

Fun Football Fact:
Owner George Halas is responsible for the name. In 1922, after he purchased the team, he decided that since one of the city's baseball teams was known as the "Cubs" and baseball players were generally smaller in size than football players, then his team should be called the "Bears."

Fun Football Fact:
What relevance does the year 1899 and Chris O'Brien have in NFL history?

Fun Football Fact:
In 1899, in Chicago, Chris O'Brien formed a neighborhood team, which he named the Morgan Athletic Club. Later, the team's name was changed to the Normals. Sometime later, their name was once again changed to the Racine Cardinals. The team eventually underwent numerous name changes, evolving from the Racine Cardinals to the Chicago Cardinals, then to the St. Louis Cardinals and then the Phoenix Cardinals.

In 1994, the team whose original name was once the Morgan Athletic Club, finally became the Arizona Cardinals and continues to operate as the oldest ongoing business in professional football.

simply, "I want to talk to you." After getting off the phone, she became very introspective and began interpreting what she thought he had meant by this comment. Since they hadn't seen each other in a few weeks, she was already feeling insecure. This lengthening separation from him, coupled with the fact that he said that he wanted to "talk" to her rather than "see" her, caused her to think that he didn't want to see her anymore.

It turned out that he didn't mean anything by his statement. He had only stated the facts and not given any thought to the history of his words. He simply wanted to talk to her more in-depth sometime in the future, since they hadn't had much time together in the weeks prior.

He didn't have a great deal of time that day or even that week, as he had expressed to her on the phone, so he already knew that he couldn't see her. Even so, he still wanted to touch base with her that day, even if he didn't have time for an in-depth conversation. She had interpreted his words by relying on her emotion instead of thinking about the facts. Additionally she had indexed his words based on his past word history use with her.

He had taken the opposite approach and didn't remember his word history and simply thought with facts instead. Since he flung the ball of communication into the air with a "Hail Mary," assuming that she would catch it without any need for specifics, she wasn't certain how to react, became anxious and dropped the ball instead of receiving it.

In communication, it is extremely important that neither party assumes anything, as you can see by the example above, in order to avoid a "dead ball." It is also vitally important in any relationship that each party makes sure that they have understood the "ball" that has been thrown to them, thereby avoiding any misunderstandings.

Women (and men), if you are unsure of something that has been said to you, and have been thrown a "Hail Mary," reconfirm the facts with your partner so he or she can clear up anything that may have been misunderstood. A good way for the woman in the example above to have handled this quandary, avoiding her anxious condition and a possible fight, would have been to ask her partner for a time when they could see each other once he got back. Advice for the man: Make the time, even if you are busy, for your mate and always remember your word history. This man was gone on a business trip, but that does not excuse him from making time during his extensive absence to at least have a quality conversation on the phone with her a few times a week.

Word Histories: Learning to Better Understand Your Team

I've written several statements regarding word histories and how they affect the passing and receiving of everyday words, yet what does this expression mean? You may have heard the phrase "word history" used only when describing the origin of a word, whether Latin or Greek, and the factual background relating to words used in an every day dictionary.

I however do not use it for that purpose alone, but have set it up as a way to remember and understand how and why certain words, when used consistently with or by our partners and those around us, affect us. As you read further, you will become familiar with what the phrase actually means when used in the context of this book.

Word histories, as defined by my language code, are the meanings we assign to each word in our vocabulary based on past experiences and our own personal belief system. A word history is our own private dictionary of assigned meanings to particular words and phrases. It is also the way we index certain words and phrases based on the continual use by those around us. Because of this, a word used by one person does not necessarily have the same meaning, implications or impact as when the same word is used by another individual. The same applies to the recipient of the word.

What the recipient hears and understands may have an entirely different impact, interpretation or power than that of another recipient. This is something that we have all seen throughout our lives as well as in the real life examples presented within this book.

A simple example of a word history commonly used, and the variances in meanings when used by different individuals, is that of the word "love." When a woman tells her best friend, in this case another woman, "I love you," it does not mean that she wants to start a long term relationship with her friend other than the platonic one that they have already established.

Generally, this word signals to the best friend that her friend really appreciates her and will be there for her no matter what struggles come their way. These same words, when used by a mother or father to their children, represent a profound love that no one can really explain. Rather, their use is an expression of the deepest kind and touches a place inside their hearts that can't be pushed aside.

When the words "I love you" are used between partners, it's the signal of a deep commitment and involves that euphoric feeling

Fun Football Fact:
Which quarterback became the first in NFL history to throw 4,000 yards in a single season?

associated with the chemicals of love spoken of in a later chapter. When a couple says the words "I love you," they have generally moved beyond the realm of dating. This simple, yet intense statement bonds them together more powerfully and usually holds a deep physical connection as well. Personal word histories are harder to determine unless you know the person well and have been involved in their life for a while. Even so, by looking at some other more universal examples of word histories, it may be easier to understand those that are more personal.

When a parent talks to a child about discipline and warns the child of the consequences if they do what they have been told not to do, that child builds up a word history in their mind, based on what the parent has said and the actions that followed. If a parent tells their child not to play with the porcelain figurines on the fireplace mantle or the child will receive a spanking, the child initially understands that there is a connection between action and consequence. Let's say that the same child decides that they are going to play with the porcelain figurines anyway and then drops and breaks one of them. If the parent follows through with the spanking, the child will know that the word "spanking" means "my bottom hurts after I do something I wasn't supposed to."

However, if the parent does not follow through with the spanking on a consistent basis, simply yelling at the child instead, the child would interpret the word "spanking" to mean the act of being yelled at. In the future, whenever the child hears the word "spanking," they will expect someone to yell at them and not hit their bottom. They have now indexed that phrase with their own personal word history, based on actions that followed the words. What happens if that child then goes over to their aunt and uncle's house for the weekend and the aunt and uncle really do administer spankings when that word "spanking" is used? The child is once again warned not to do something or they will receive a spanking.

The child's word history signals to them that they will receive only a bit of yelling and then they can continue with their behavior. When the aunt and uncle follow through with an actual spanking, the child is shocked, screaming more out of surprise than pain. Their word history has now been shattered and their belief system altered.

Confusion may set in regarding what the child believes will happen when the word "spanking" is used in reference to discipline. If the child consistently goes to their aunt and uncle's house and they consistently spank the child after they have warned the child

Fun Football Fact:
On December 24, 1967, Joe Namath, quarterback for the New York Jets, became the first player in NFL history to throw 4,000 yards in a single season. He made his landmark pass in a game against the San Diego Chargers. His passing yards that season totaled 4007!

not to do something and the child still does it, the child will then have a word history with them that differs from that of their parent. The word history will be as follows: "When Mom or Dad tell me not to do something or I will receive a spanking and then I do it anyway, spanking means I get yelled at." "However, when Aunt Lilian or Uncle John tell me not to do something, spanking means that my bottom will hurt if I misbehave." Are you beginning to understand my usage of the phrase "word history?"

Let me use a more passive and very common example. A friend of yours consistently writes, "I'll talk to you later," when writing the exit line in an e-mail or when leaving a message on your voicemail, but then never actually calls or comes over to talk to you later. You, as the recipient, will eventually know that the phrase has no other meaning than a simple goodbye because there is no action actually associated with those words.

Your word history now associates these particular words with a lack of action. Basically, a pattern has now been set and you have indexed that phrase accordingly. What would happen if, after years of using this exit line, your friend actually called a little bit later and said to you, "I told you that I would talk to you later and so here I am." You would be a bit surprised, wouldn't you?

Fun Football Fact:
What event took place on March 20, 1984?

Here's another example. You tell the woman in your life that you will "see her later in the week." Every week, you say the same thing to her after the weekend and every week, without fail, you come over at 8 PM on Wednesday. After several weeks, your girl-friend now has it engrained in her word history that your words "I'll see you later in the week" now mean that every week on Wednesday at 8 PM, she will see you. She naturally comes to rely on that fact.

If you don't show up until 9 PM one week, she may be a little worried but doesn't want to nag so she doesn't say anything. She just assumes that something happened to detain you. She may even ask you why you were late, but she most likely wouldn't make a big deal of it because it was just one time. However, when the next week comes and you have told her again that you will "see her later in the week," but don't show up on Wednesday at 8 PM as usual, she begins to worry that something happened to you and calls. This time, you are at home, on the couch, relaxing and she's a little annoyed that you tell her you will see her on Friday.

You have now caused confusion and conflict in her word history with you, i.e., the way she has indexed your usage of those particular words and that phrase. Because in the past, you had consistently had an action associated with that phrase, that of coming over every Wednesday at 8 PM, she expected the same behavior to continue.

When that changed and you did not follow with the actions you had always taken in the past, you have caused a break in her word history with you. The affect of the uncertainty of your words and actions, may be beginning to sow the seeds of anxiety about the relationship in her mind if the matter is not discussed and resolved.

In order to completely understand each other's word histories, we have to "key" into the people around us. The way people initially react to our words have nothing at all to do with us initially, but are rather shaped by other relationships in their past. Once they get to know us, they form new word histories with us based on our responses and subsequent actions. Therefore, we need to remember how they reacted to the words we used and to the actions we took; we also need to identify the words they used and the actions that followed. Remember that those word histories will help us remain consistent in our interactions with those who are in our lives and help to stave off any confusion or hurt that may result and could lead to disruptive arguments.

Misunderstandings are a huge part of relational fighting. Therefore, not only do both parties need to understand the facts, but each party must also try to remember the history behind their words in order to avoid such misunderstandings in the future. *"If it is possible, as far as it depends on you, live at peace with everyone." Romans 12:18*

Foster good will in your relationships and remember your word history.

Fun Football Fact: Wellington Mara was named president of the NFC on March 20, 1984.

CHAPTER 5
Learning to Key—Women Feel Their Words, Hear Them

A well-trained and observant football player can "key" on his opponent by carefully watching for subtle movements and turns, allowing him to anticipate his opponent's next move and block or intercept more effectively. While I am not suggesting that your partner is your opponent (although sometimes it does feel that way), if you also carefully observe your partners movements, their tone of voice and their words, you may be able to block or intercept any miscommunication that could lead to long-term problems.

Recently, while watching the movie *City Of Angels*, I noticed a key point that rang true for me. This portrayal presented such an accurate depiction of the lines of communication and how we perceive and interpret them in our very unique and different ways.

In the story, Maggie's boyfriend, Jordan, had planned a trip to Lake Tahoe but she didn't want to go. Instead, she was trying to make him understand that she only wanted to spend time together with him. He didn't understand because, to him, the act of going to Lake Tahoe was spending time together. All she wanted to do was sit, be still and spend time together. He couldn't conceive what she was talking about, so the following conversation took place:

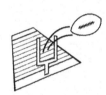

Fun Football Fact:
Who holds the record for the most consecutive passes without an interception?

> *Maggie:* No. No. No. Let's just stand here for five minutes with nothing but ourselves.
>
> *Jordan:* What am I supposed to do?

At that point, he stared blankly at her, trying to accommodate her wishes but not really understanding the task. Later in the film, he again tried to do what she had earlier asked of him: to spend time with her. Unfortunately, he took the act of "spending time" quite literally, while she meant it to be on an emotional level. She was sitting in the doctors' locker room when he came in and sat in front of her.

Maggie: What are you doing?

Jordan: (Staring at her with an intent and comical side-glance and pronouncing very methodically): I'm spending time together.

As he made this statement, his chin slowly descended towards his chest with each word. It was not only a very funny moment in the film, but it also definitely hit the mark as to how we perceive and understand each other's language. He obviously thought that she meant just sitting there would accommodate her needs for spending time together and he was trying to accommodate this need in a way that he thought was important to her. To him, spending time together was going on a trip or watching a movie. To her, just "being," simply sitting still or holding one another, was most important. He seemed to misinterpret that "foreign" concept, though, attempting to simply sit with her in the doctors' locker room. Moreover, to Maggie, spending time together was more about having a meaningful conversation.

Jordan didn't understand because Maggie was thinking from the "right-brain" perspective of relational issues and he was thinking from the more factual "left-brain" point of view. It was not part of Jordan's internal software to understand that Maggie wanted to "feel" spending time together, while he wanted to literally "spend time together" by doing something. She wanted emotional bonding, not travel or action but simply sitting and talking intimately with each other. This reinforces the literal meaning of the word "feel," which is to "undergo the experience. [ix]" Women need and crave intimate communication just as an athlete needs to warm up his muscles before going on the field. If you remember this point, you will be scoring many touchdowns in your relationships. Forget it and you will be punting time and time again.

Feeling Words—More on Women's Language

How can you learn to "key" into the facts and emotions that are part of a woman's syntax? First, listen intently to what your partner says. "Hear" the words and then analyze them as you would a new play formation that your coach has given you to work on. Look up the words that your partner uses to find the possible meaning behind each one and take into account her personal word history or what you know of it thus far.

I know that this seems like a lot of work, but being on any team that is going to the Super Bowl requires effort, hard work and diligence. The payoff in the end is well worth it. Just ask any player who has made it to the Super Bowl and you will know that the rewards can be endless.

I believe that when you hear something, see it and can touch it, it makes a greater impact. When you look up a word that you've heard, even if you already know its meaning, you will not only have heard the word, but also visually seen it. Then, by touching the dictionary, you will have also added the sense of touch. All of this will have a greater impact on the meaning of the word. (By the way, looking up words in the dictionary has an added bonus for those people who are poor spellers. This simple technique will increase your spelling accuracy immensely.)

Women use a lot of feeling words, something that "left-brain" individuals may not always understand because they deal primarily with facts. Since women feel their words, the words that you choose to communicate with your mate will last, even if your relationship does not. She will remember what you said to her and it can have a deep and lasting effect on her emotional well-being. Remember that she is temporally aware. A few feeling words that are quite powerful emotionally are caring, felt, touched, hurt, happy, disappointed, and upset. Let me use a few of these words in the sentences of a "right-brain" individual.

In the following example, Mary is talking to her boyfriend, who asks her about her day at work. Mary responds: "Today at the office, I heard a few of the girls talking about a cat they had found outside the door this morning. The cat apparently was hungry and looked emaciated. They also said it looked as though someone had intentionally hurt her. When I walked over to join in their conversation, they began relating to me the story of how they had found her. I felt so bad. It upset me most of the day to think that someone could be so cruel to an animal. I wish I could find a way to stop all cruelty to animals!"

To a "right-brain" individual, this is a perfectly sound and easy conversation to understand. To a "left-brain" individual, however, it may be hard to relate to the facts. He may wonder what the point of

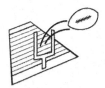

Fun Football Fact: Bernie Kosar holds the record for the most consecutive passes without an interception. His total? 308!

the story is in relation to the original topic of how her day went. The man may want to know where the story is going to lead and how he can solve the problem of animal cruelty for his partner. He may not really understand what this has to do with how her day went and may not fully realize that this event really did affect her entire day.

"Left-brain" individuals want the facts, not the emotions. The "feeling" words that Mary used in the story would have helped her boyfriend, had he understood how these words really did describe the way Mary's day went. A "right-brain" individual like Mary is not only making a statement about her day, but about how the plight of the cat made her feel and how it emotionally affected her day.

Because her boyfriend is a "left-brained" individual whose wonderful chemical gift from birth is to discover facts and solve, i.e. conquer problems, Mary's response to his question may have left him thinking that she is looking for a solution. He may wonder if that's why Mary brought up the cat in the first place.

However, she was not necessarily looking for a solution but rather wanted to express her day in emotional terms, which the story of the cat represented. If the conversation about the cat had continued for much longer, Mary's boyfriend, being a "left-brain" individual as well as suffering from a lack of hard facts, might have lost his concentration.

Now, let me show you the meaning of each of the feeling words from the conversation example that I gave above. It may help you to gain more perspective as to how a woman may feel when each word is used and why the cat really did affect Mary's day.

Fun Football Fact:
When did the Pro Football Hall of Fame gather the most living members together at one time?

Hungry:	"The discomfort, weakness, or pain caused by a lack of food. [x]"
Emaciated:	"To make or become extremely thin, especially from starvation. [xi]"
Hurt:	"To feel or cause to feel pain. [xii]"
Felt:	"Feel. [xiii]"
Upset:	"To distress mentally or emotionally. [xiv]"
Cruel:	"Causing suffering; pain. [xv]"

As you can see by each of their definitions, these are powerful words. As stated earlier, a "right-brain" individual actually feels these words and there are emotions attached to each one of them. They can't help it because it's the way their brain is wired. It's important that they are this way so that they can care for and nurture those around them.

Why do you think that so many women cry when watching *Ever After, While You Were Sleeping* and *Where the Heart Is*, or when reading *Readers Digest*? It's because they develop a relationship with the characters and they actually identify and relate to the words used within the plot. They actually feel what they think the character feels based on the portrayal.

A side note for women asking the same question to the men in their life about how their day went. I recommend that if you want to find out how your partner's day went and what events took place, instead of asking him, "How was your day?" ask him, "So, what happened in your day, dear?" Why do I say this? While the first sentence requires your partner to use feeling words to answer and may not carry any resonance to the "left-brain" thinker who doesn't think of work in emotional terms, the second asks simply for the facts. It relates more clearly to the way in which a "left-brain" person would think.

Fun Football Fact: On July 28, 2000, over 100 of the 136 living members of the Pro Football Hall of Fame gathered to celebrate in Canton, Ohio.

By contrast, because women see their work as part of their family activity and it actually helps to define who they are as individuals, feeling words are appropriate for describing a woman's day. When you ask a man how his day was, he may answer "Fine," "Good," or "Okay." These are appropriate answers for a "left-brain" individual in response to your "feeling" question. At the same time, he may also feel like you're interrogating him or even think that you are ambushing him. If you ask him about the events that happened during his day, he is then dealing with facts instead of feelings, reason versus emotions and you are much more likely to receive an in-depth answer.

For men, I realize that women's stories tend to go on and on and you wonder when the end is coming. You want just the facts, and are looking for a conclusion. I often hear men saying to the women in their life to "Speed it up."; "And the point is?"; "Can you give me the short version?" and so on. To help you avoid being sacked, try to think of her conversation as you would a football game you are about to partake in. When the coach reveals to the players his game strategies, a lot of detail goes into explaining the "plan" that will give them the final outcome of a victory.

The same is true for a woman. When she is going on and on in a story, giving you every single detail you wish you had never heard, remember that she is driving her story to the end zone for the ultimate goal of a victory to get her point across.

A very wise and wonderful man in my life is acutely aware of this when dealing with his daughter. He once told me, "She has all these emotions, and she has to get them out before she gets her point across." Because he has been able to get past her emotions, he has been able to actually "hear" her go on and on until she reaches the end of her stories without a lot of frustration on his part.

Here is a funny example of men using facts to relay information to a woman and the same situation reversed, a women using the same facts but mixed with emotional descriptor words to come to the same conclusion. I am certain that many of you reading this book can absolutely relate to this scenario, that of giving directions. Now, with the advent of mapping programs and GPS systems, it's no longer necessary to give manual directions, but let me give you a few examples from both a "right" and a "left-brain" individual.

A "right-brain" individual asks a "left-brain" individual how to get to the coffee shop they are going to meet at later in the day. The "left-brain" individual states the following: "Go to the intersection of 8th and 1st street, approximately one mile from your house. Take a left on 1st street heading north. Once you are on 1st street, at the first stop light, take a left on Hormel Ave. Go three tenths of a mile on Hormel Ave until you reach the intersection of Hormel Ave. and Hunter Street. Take a right on Hunter Street and the Brand X coffee shop will be on your left."

Now let me give you directions from a "right-brain" individual to the same destination: "Go out of your driveway and turn left. Proceed to the intersection of 8th and 1st street (you'll see Brand Z gas station on the left corner and Brand Y gas station on the right corner. There is also a strip mall to the left of 8th street and a yogurt shop on 1st street).

Take a left on 1st street heading North (As you head down 1st street, you will also see a large Dress shop and The Brand T coffee shop on your right. This is NOT the coffee shop). Once you are on 1st street, at the first stop light (there is Brand M gas station on the left corner and a nice Chinese restaurant on the opposite corner), take a left on Hormel Ave. Go about a city block on Hormel Ave until you reach the first large intersection on Hormel Ave.

There's a Brand A hair shop on the corner of Hormel and there's a Brand D donut shop of the corner of Hunter. (If you pass

Brand S grocery store, you have gone too far. Go back.) Take a right on Hunter Street and the Brand X coffee shop will be on your left right next to the Smart and Save shop. There is also a U Take and Bake pizzeria on the right of the coffee shop."

During a recent trip to Lake Tahoe with an outdoor club I am involved with, this scenario played out before me. I watched as a woman was giving directions to a man with a lot of descriptors in it. He looked a little annoyed. Meanwhile, off to the side, I noticed several of her male friends mimicking her saying, "Yes, take a right at the small green bush they have just chopped the top off of and a left at the purple car with four doors." In the end everyone was laughing, but it was a very funny example of the above scenario I listed.

Caution Is Paramount

It's important that you are very careful and selective in your choice of words when dealing with a "right-brain" individual. The words you use will have a profound effect on them. When the coach for the Seattle Seahawks decides which plays he is going to use for each game, he carefully and methodically chooses them according to which opposing team he is playing against that week.

If he uses the wrong plays, it will affect the outcome of the game and possibly the entire season. Each opponent warrants a different set of strategies if his team is going to win. While adjustments can be made during the game, he has already given any backup plans careful consideration. When dealing with "right-brain" individuals, you must also choose wisely which "plays," or words, you will use. When the brain and the body feel something, they commit that feeling to memory, so it's vital to link words with positive feelings.

If you want to get to the Super Bowl, this is one of the most important lessons that you must learn: watch your words. If you don't, you will make a fatal error that could cost you the game. If you lose too many games, you won't be going to the Super Bowl.

Fun Football Fact:
Why did NBC pull the plug during the last minutes of the New York Jets vs. Oakland Raiders game on November 17, 1968?

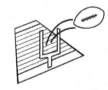

Fun Football Fact:
NBC cut off the last minute of the New York Jets vs. Oakland Raiders because they wanted to ensure that their children's special Heidi aired on time. In the final forty-two seconds of the game, however, the Oakland Raiders scored two times for a 43 - 32 victory!

CHAPTER 6
Hitch and Go Doesn't Work
in Relationships
Do What You Say, Say What You Do

While a "Hitch and Go" is an acceptable play on the football field, it is considered an "illegal procedure" in a relationship. While faking a quick turn to catch a pass and then continuing downfield for a deeper one may throw off your opponent and score points with your teammates on a real field, it will only cause anger and hostility in a relationship.

If you want a fulfilling and lasting relationship with a woman, you must match what you have committed in words to her with your actions. People will often say something that they fully intend to follow through on and then forget about it completely. This will eventually lead to a lot of penalties on the playing field of love.

What I heard resoundingly on the surveys I conducted with men and women over a course of a year and a half was: "Don't say it if you don't mean it! Actions speak louder than words!" What you commit to someone with your words and then how you actually respond and react to the words you have used, reveal a lot about your character.

Let's pretend that you are the quarterback for the San Francisco 49ers. The initial play chosen by the coach and discussed in the huddle was to pass the ball. But, you have decided to proceed with an audible and carry it yourself instead, without a valid reason or any logic backing your decision for calling an audible. You are probably looking at a loss because you would be confusing your team and they wouldn't know how to back you up.

While there's a chance that they may pick up on the new play after a moment, you have just caused confusion amongst the other

Fun Football Fact:
Who holds the record
for the most
consecutive games
lost?

members of your team and perhaps sown discontent, especially if the new play fails. With that split-second decision, you changed the plan and quite possibly cost your team possession of the ball.

While calling an audible may occasionally be an accepted practice, if you consistently call them, you will eventually be traded or kicked off the team because no one will be able to rely on you. You will no longer have your team's trust. Since a "team" is defined as a "group organized to work together, [xvi]" you are in a relationship with your team and must work together. If you want your team to back you up, you need to be there for them and follow through with the correct calls at the right time. In the same way, if you want your relationship to work, you need to follow through and make your actions match your words. You must communicate and follow through with that communication or trust will dwindle. If this happens, you may want to call a time-out and regroup. To be the star quarterback of your relationship, you must be self-critical and objective, as well as consistent and reliable. There is no "Hitch and Go" when it comes to relationships and communication!

Fun Football Fact:
The Chicago Cardinals hold the record for the most consecutive games lost, 19, set during the period from 1942 to 1945!

Avoid a Turnover—Jesting Isn't Funny

Since women feel their words, don't joke with them about who they are or what they look like. Women take things much more personally than men do. While you may have been joking, she may take it as a personal assault. There is a fine line between having a sense of humor and causing a disturbance in the balance of what someone believes about himself or herself. Laughter is great and someone who has a good sense of humor and can laugh at himself or herself is a joy to be around. Someone who laughs "at" someone else, instead of "with" someone else, however, is another story entirely. Repeated behavior like this will cause a "turnover" in your relationship and you will definitely lose the game.

Let me give you an example of when a man's words may cross over the line in this regard. On several occasions, I have passed by a pregnant woman while her husband was making a seemingly innocent comment to or about her, including things like, "Oh this is my plump little dumpling! She has a bun in the oven."

To a woman, being called a "plump dumpling" definitely implies that she's fat, even if he is only proud of her pregnancy. Even unintentionally implying that she's fat is a "personal foul" and a fifteen-yard penalty for you!

Fun Football Fact:
Who is considered the NFL's "star" wide receiver of all time?

In the same vein, I also once heard a man saying, "Make room please" along with a grand gesturing of his arms as he escorted his pregnant wife through a room. His wife's face was not that of a happy woman! Yet another personal foul and another fifteen-yard penalty! While her husband thought that he was being polite and careful with his wife because he was "making room" for her, she probably interpreted his words to understand that he believed that she was fat. If she weren't fat, she reasoned, he wouldn't have to make room for her. Not only is a pregnant woman more acutely sensitive because of the extra hormones running through her body, she is also, being a woman, naturally one who feels words: a double whammy.

A better way to make any of the previous statements is to put it as follows: "This is my beautiful wife. Isn't she the most beautiful and radiant woman you have ever seen? She's carrying our baby." While you say it, touch her face and hold her hand. Try it and see how much more positively she responds to you.

Your words and your touch will make her feel that she is the only woman in the world for you and you just scored a touchdown by pointing out the fact that she is pregnant. This implies that you think no one can tell she's pregnant, which also implies that you don't see her as being large. Bonus! Touching her at the same time will implant the memory in her senses more deeply and will engrain your words in her word history. Now you have made the successful placekick, earning the extra point!

More Extra Points Compliments Go a Long Way

A compliment, as with a smile, costs you nothing, but will gain you a lot of extra points. It's Friday night and you have asked a woman out to a nice restaurant and to go dancing. On the first date, a woman most likely will not ask you what you think of her outfit. If you want to get the first down without any penalties and gain extra yardage, tell her she looks great!

Let's change the scenario to a time when you have been dating a woman for a while. Once she gets to know you, she may begin to ask you what you think of the outfit that she is wearing and how she looks in it. What do you do if you don't particularly like the outfit that she's wearing? While honesty in a relationship is very important, you may want to huddle up with yourself and find the best play for the situation.

Fun Football Fact:
Jerry Rice of the Oakland Raiders is the star wide receiver of all time! He has made 196 touchdowns in his career! Here are his stats:

Jersey #80
Height: 6'2"
Weight: 200 lbs.
Birth Date: 10/13/1962
College he attended: Mississippi Valley State
Years in the NFL: 19!

G	GS	Rec	Yrds
270	255	1456	21597

Avg	LG	TD
14.8	96t	196

Some of the Records Jerry Rice has Broken:
Jim Brown's NFL record of 126 touchdowns. Art Monk's NFL record of 940 receptions. James Lofton's NFL record of 14,004 receiving yards. Steve Largent's NFL record of 100 touchdown receptions.

Awards:
Too numerous to mention! Just about everything imaginable!

Unless she is in the first stages of preparation for the evening or in the process of buying the outfit in a store and wants your opinion as to whether she should purchase it or not, she has already bought the outfit and thinks that she looks good in it. Nobody purchases an outfit because they think that they look bad in it!

If she is standing before you in the "finished product" and asking that question, she has clearly dressed that way because she thought that you would enjoy looking at her. Generally speaking, it was more of a rhetorical question that was expecting a compliment to follow rather than a sincere plea for advice. This is where "keying" on her will come into play in a big way.

If you want to gain extra yards and a possible touchdown later in the evening, you had better say that she looks great! Whether you have only dated her a few times or you have been married to her for fifty years, a woman wants and needs to know that the man she is with finds her attractive, just as you need that same validation from her. Simply put, she spent time thinking about and preparing for the evening with you, which means that she thinks she looks good or else that wouldn't have been her final choice. She wants you to tell her that she looks good, regardless of whether or not you, as a visual male, would have chosen that look for her.

She wants you to look past the reality of what you see and step into the world of what she sees. She wants you to see past the bulge that may be sticking out on her hips with the dress that she has chosen and see the way she feels inside and what she sees at that moment in the mirror -- beauty!

Don't mishandle the ball and risk a fumble by telling her that you don't like the outfit. That will be a huge turn-over for you! The words you choose will have an emotional impact on her and she will remember that incident for a long time. If you really don't like the outfit she is wearing, a more acceptable statement would be a suggestion such as the following (however, use it with caution and make sure she was really asking for your opinion):

Try saying, "You are beautiful no matter what you wear!" Then, walk up to her, put your arms around her and say, "However, if you really are asking what my favorite outfit on you is, I'll tell you. It's that beautiful black dress you wore a few weeks ago. That dress makes you look even more stunning than you are right now."

Having said this, give her a short passionate kiss. With this behavior, you are validating the way she hopes you feel about her by telling her that she is ravishing at that moment, but you are also expressing your feelings for an outfit that you love to see her in.

No matter what she chooses to do after that, you will need to support her and drop the subject. Whatever you do, even if you don't get her into the outfit of your choice, don't tell her that you want her to change. If you press her on this, you might as well throw in the towel, forfeit the game and spend the night alone watching a movie on your couch! While she may not say anything to you initially, she will hold it in her heart and you may not gain any more yards during that night!

CHAPTER 7
The Huddle—Emotional Word Pictures

Prior to the "snap," the players huddle together to go over the play they will be using during this down. They create an image in their mind, using familiar words, to try and work down the field towards a touchdown.

An emotional word picture works with the same concept. An emotional word picture builds a scenario, using familiar words, with the goal of scoring points and making a communication touchdown when other attempts have failed. An emotional word picture is a story that incorporates something familiar and/or well loved by the person you are trying to have an impact on. When emotions have an impact on us, that impact engages the right side of the brain, helping us to understand what is being said to us more clearly as well as committing it to our memory. We take in a lot of information during that time, and many of our senses are stimulated.

Basically an emotional word picture activates the listener or readers emotions as well as engaging their intellect. When these two components work together, it will cause the listener or reader to not merely listen to our words, but experience them and better comprehend what we are trying to communicate.

An emotional word picture taps into the part of the brain that causes us to not only remember from, but feel from. Essentially it uses simple every day items to create a more complex imagery that draws the listener or reader in. The words, statements, or stories used, will immediately create a picture in the listener's or readers mind that will convey and clarify more preciously what you are trying to communicate to them.

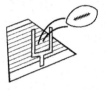

Fun Football Fact:
When was the first
time that sudden
death overtime was
initiated?

While there is usually only one player in the emotional word picture huddle, mapping out which words will have the most effective and quickest impact, the planned end result is the same - a communication touchdown.

Women, listen up. While this chapter pertains to men as well, women are more likely to feel as if they are not "getting through" to the men in their lives. In order to better enable the man in your life to understand you, you will need to create an emotional word picture for him as well as learn to relate to him in the world of facts instead of emotions.

We use simple emotional word pictures every day in sentences like: "That looks like a crisp, juicy apple." If someone says that phrase, it instantly draws a picture in the listeners or readers mind that causes them to think about and remember a crisp juicy apple they once had. They will instantaneously remember how nice it tasted, the juice that may have squirted into their mouth when they first bit into it and the sound of the crunch when their teeth sunk into the skin. That's a simple example of an emotional word picture.

Here is another example: "The smell of the lasagna baking is driving me crazy! I can almost taste the oozing cheese and rich sauce." For those people who love, or perhaps just like lasagna, your mouth begins to water with this set of words.

Here's a more powerful emotional word picture. "I love you." That one, simple phrase alone is probably the most powerful of all emotional word pictures. That one "simple" yet complex phrase, can conjure up a myriad of different scenarios and thoughts.

As previously stated, when said to one partner by another, it wells up deep emotions within their beings and the words "forever" or "I do" may pop into one or the other partners' brain. When said by parent to a child, a warm feeling of safety and home envelope the child. What about the emotional word picture, "Build a bridge and get over it!"? This one phrase completely conveys the emotions of the person who is delivering it. Each of these basic emotional word pictures evokes its own particular feeling.

Emotional word pictures can have a powerful and profound impact on the relationships in our lives when trying to make someone understand our feelings or a particular point of view. To create an emotional word picture you will need to do a little research. You need to find out what items in your partners world they favor. Things they love, situations that have had an impact on their lives, and people who they hold dear.

It is these items, situations and people that will allow you to create a story, much like the creative writing papers you were required to write in English 101 while in High School or College. In the same way, you are creating a story using these items to build imagery.

For people who cook, think of it like a recipe card. You have been given all the ingredients, e.g. objects, situations and people, from the research you have done and now it's time to mix them together and bake them into a food item the person you are trying to reach can not only digest, but want to take into their brain to process. Let me share an example of an emotional word picture that I created for a boyfriend a few years ago. I was amazed at the impact it had on him. A few of his favorite things were trains, Pepsi, and reading the newspaper.

The relationship between my boyfriend and me was strained, at least for me. Despite the fact that I had spoken with him numerous times regarding my need to be with him, not just around him, I wasn't able to break through the communication gap. For him, however, the relationship was fine, and he didn't understand why I felt differently. Since all of my efforts failed, I decided to try a new technique I had learned called an emotional word picture.

Here is what I told him: "Imagine you're about to take a trip on the Orient Express. You get to the loading dock and the baggage handler offers to take your bag onboard. You tell him, 'No thanks, I can handle it myself.' The baggage handler shrugs his shoulders and walks away. Once inside the train, you see beautiful and plush surroundings. The seats are covered in velvet, the floor has beautiful Oriental carpets strewn across it, the tables are set with fine china and linen and the walls are covered with rare paintings.

The host offers to find a comfortable seat for you, but you tell him that you can find one on your own. Once seated, the waiter comes over to offer you a newspaper and a beverage while you are waiting for the train to depart. You order a Pepsi and begin to read the newspaper. The waiter comes back with a Pepsi in a beautiful crystal glass. He tries to make conversation with you, but instead of responding to him, you reach around the newspaper and take the glass from his tray.

Throughout the trip, various people try to engage you in conversation. You politely acknowledge them, but do not converse. Instead, you quickly return to your newspaper. Each time someone approaches you to offer some sort of service, you politely brush them off and return to reading.

Each person walks away, saddened that you're not interested in their services. They are there to make your ride on the Orient Express a pleasurable one, but you won't let them. As you read through each section of the newspaper, you toss it on the ground. You spill your Pepsi on the linen and the carpets, but never acknowledge or even thank the staff that cleans the mess up for you. The staff members in your car sit huddled in the corner waiting for you to let them serve you and each one has an expression of sorrow on his/her face. When the ride is over, you leave your trash scattered throughout the car and exit without so much as a goodbye.

Now imagine that the Orient Express is my heart and the staff is me. You have thrown your garbage all over my heart without thinking about how it might hurt me. I want to do things for you and talk with you, but you read your newspaper, drink your Pepsi and leave me sad and alone in the corner because you haven't recognized all that I have to give to you. You tell me that you can do everything yourself then leave a mess for me to clean up."

There was more to my word picture, but you get the general idea. I was greatly surprised at the lasting impact that my emotional word picture had on our relationship. He was able to feel the words because they were intertwined with objects that he favored. Since he was able to feel the words, he was also able to understand my need for more interaction with him and he was able to make a change.

Creating an emotional word picture can be hard in the beginning. However, if you take the time to think about the things that your partner enjoys doing, the food he or she loves, their favorite places and other images that are close to him or her, you will be able to incorporate them into a piece that will help to convey the messages of your heart and mind. If you would like to gain yardage, avoid a sudden death and stop season ending injuries from taking place in your relationship, emotional word pictures are an invaluable tool.

Fun Football Fact:
The first time that the sudden death over-time rule was used was on August 28, 1955, during a pre-season game between the St. Louis Rams and the New York Giants. Three minutes into overtime, the St. Louis Rams defeated the New York Giants 23 - 17.

CHAPTER 8
Getting Benched—The Difference Between a Man's "No" and a Woman's "No"

Fun Football Fact:
When was the NFL's first night game played?

The simplest part of the male language code includes the words "yes" and "no." At least in my experience and research thus far, I've found that when a "left-brain" individual says "no," he actually means "no;" at the same time, "yes" actually means "yes."

Women however, are more complex. A woman's "yes" can mean "yes," but a woman's "no" can mean a multitude of other things, not the least of which is that she really wants you to ask her again. This may in part be because she wants to feel like you really want her to do what you initially asked her to do - it boosts her ego to be asked twice. A "no" from a woman can also mean that she is trying to be polite and not interfere with something that you had planned. So, to be politically correct, she says "no" when she actually wants to say "yes."

As a man, you have to become very adept as to which "no" is actually negative and which "no" simply means, "Ask me again!" If you want to score points in a situation like this, you need to make her feel like you really want her there and that she is not taking away from any of the festivities, but is, in fact, adding to them. Many times, if you ask her one more time, it will satisfy her and she will decline, going away feeling loved and wanted. The choices you make in this instance will either gain you the full six points for a touchdown and a chance at a conversion or will see you fumble the ball and end up on the bench. If you fumble the ball too often, you may get benched permanently!

Fun Football Fact:
The NFL's first night game was played on November 6, 1929. The teams that played that night were the Chicago Cardinals and the Providence Steam Roller at Kinsley Park, which was a minor-league baseball field. Floodlights were set up twenty feet above the grass and the football was painted white so that it would be visible in the night sky. The Cardinals won the Steam Roller's in a shut out game. The score? 16 - 0!

Monday Night Football

Its Monday night and you want to invite a few of the guys over to your house to watch the Cincinnati Bengals play the Pittsburgh Steelers. You ask your girlfriend if she would like to watch the game with you and your buddies and join in the group activities.

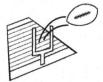

Fun Football Fact:
What team holds the record for the most fumbles in one season?

She feels like she may be interrupting valuable male bonding time with you and your friends and doesn't want to interfere, so she politely says, "No." Secretly, she would love to sit with you, enjoy the game and get to know your buddies, but externally, she is playing the sacrificial martyr by telling you, "No. thank you."

You, as a "left-brain" individual, think that her "no" actually meant "no," so you reply, "Okay honey, have a good evening." At that point, you think the matter is closed. Most women would never make an issue of it and would act as though the matter was closed. However, some women may be a little hurt that you didn't ask them again. In that instance, had you asked her again, you would have gained a lot of yardage and possibly a touchdown before you reached the second down.

Even if she says "no" the second time (and generally, that "no" really means no), she will know that you wanted her to be there with you. That particular move will go down in her memory banks as extra points for you and she will retain that information for a long time. You have just added value to your love account with her and no penalty flags will be raised.

Fun Football Fact:
The San Francisco 49ers and the Chicago Bears are tied for the record with fifty-six fumbles each in one season.

Here are a few tips for learning the difference between a woman saying "no" and a woman meaning "no." If your partner says, "No thank you, honey," with a large smile on her face and then gives you a frontal hug, this means her "no" really is a "no." She's very happy that you asked her and she is fully satisfied that you really did want her there.

If your partner says "No. Thanks" without enthusiasm and then gives you a half smile or a shrug smile, you might want to take her hand and ask, "Are you sure, honey? Because I would love for you to be there." You'll be amazed at the change in her responsiveness to you, even if she still answers "no." Not only have you used a non-verbal cue by holding her hand, a very powerful action, but you have also used a feeling word in your sentence.

However, if your partner says "no" abruptly and walks away from you, something is either wrong in her world or between you and her. It's best if you stop everything and go over to give her a hug. Ask if there is something wrong and inquire whether you can help her in any way. When you do this, be prepared to actually sit and either listen or discuss the matter at hand. Don't simply shove her off, making her believe the game is more important than her, or you may get benched for the season.

Some time ago, I watched a show where they had the all-time funniest sports blooper clips. One clip I watched showed a former Chicago Bears quarterback being tackled by several of the opposing team members and inadvertently plowing the referee down as he fell. When everyone got off of the quarterback and then off of the referee, they found that the referee was still making the call, waving his hands across the field while still flattened on his back. It was quite a funny sight.

Fun Football Fact:
What player holds the career record for the most fumbles?

If you don't make the right choice when a woman says "no," you may find yourself much like the referee did in that game: on the ground, stampeded and still making the call, not knowing what really hit you. That's why it's so important that you are hearing what she is saying verbally as well as paying attention to her non-verbal cues. I feel sorry for the male species, those who must figure out a woman's hidden meanings. Even in the animal kingdom this rule applies, so don't think we plan to confuse you on purpose. It's just part of our natural genetic dialogue. So, if you can begin to understand a woman's language early on in the game, you will score more touchdowns and get hit with fewer penalties and yards lost.

If you hear a woman each time she says "no" and commit her response to your memory, you will get better at deciphering her code and learning her word history. Men are conquerors by nature, so win the game! It may take time and a lot of practice, but you will be glad you put the time and effort in when the payoff comes. If you rise to the challenge and succeed, you will make it to the Super Bowl every year!

Fun Football Fact:
Warren Moon holds the career record for most fumbles at 161.

On the flip side, I want to clearly state something now so that this particular part of the book does not get taken out of context. When a woman says "no" to sexual advances, it ALWAYS means "NO." It NEVER means "yes." There are NO "cheap shots" when a woman says "No." In this situation, "NO" is a complete sentence with no hidden meanings. "If I take care of my character, my reputation will take care of itself" - *Dwight L. Moody.*

CHAPTER 9
Making the First Round Draft Pick
with Romance

When an unknown player wants to be picked up in the first round of a draft, he does everything in his power to be noticed by the people who can make a difference in his career. If you want the woman in your life to pick you over the other players on the field, you need to set the same standards consistently in the romance game.

If you are one of those enlightened men who have romance down, congratulations! If you are like much of the male population, however, help has arrived. Perhaps when you first met the woman in your life, you did everything you could to please her and make her happy. You opened doors, picked her wildflowers, took her on long walks under the stars and much more. So what happened after that initial stage of your courtship? The answer is that you conquered her, you won her over.

On a first date, you try to impress your intended and treat her with respect, admiration and kindness. If she agrees to a second date, you obviously got the first date right or she wouldn't have consented to a second one. So when does complacency take place in a relationship? From my observation, complacency usually begins within the first three to six months after the first date. It is during this time that most men and women start to let their "hair hang loose" so to speak, and use behaviors and mannerisms that they would have deemed unsuitable or inappropriate for the first, second or even third date. Why is that? Because they believe that if these behaviors were to be introduced at the beginning of a relationship, the other person would perhaps lose interest in them. There is sound reasoning and certainly truth behind those beliefs.

While some of those behaviors are a natural part of life and can't be helped, other behaviors or even the lack of behaviors that were introduced or left out during the initial stages of courtship, can lead to trouble within the relationship. As with the word history, the behaviors and mannerisms that are introduced during the beginning of the relationship are also set up and memorized in the cells of the brain. Expectations are set during that time and if you want to continue to have the same kind of relationship you had in the beginning, you need to make sure you continue the same pattern you started out with. That's why it's best to start out by presenting exactly the person you are.

Let me give you a story to help better represent this idea. Once a week, you and your guy friends meet at the local pizzeria for Monday Night Football. Everyone splits the tab evenly and you always end up being the treasurer by default. After a few months, some of the guys start bringing their girlfriends but don't pitch in extra money to cover the expense.

When the money collected comes to you and the final tab is tallied, you are short but some of the guys have already left. After having to pitch in the extra money a few times, you become irritated and say something. The guys who have been taking advantage of your kind nature finally fork over the money but then stop coming for pizza altogether. What happened? They had a certain amount set in their minds that they paid each week and since you had covered the bill the other times, they were used to only having to pay that much and assumed there would never be any more payment due.

While this example is more about people using one another, it also shows a simple behavior pattern that occurred and when expectations weren't met, trouble set in. While I am not saying that you should let people take advantage of you financially, I use this example to show what happens when a pattern is introduced, followed consistently and then taken away.

When you first begin a relationship, you start out doing all the wonderful and romantic things you think will endear you to the other person. Once the newness of the relationship wears off, however, you naturally start taking advantage of the other person's generosity of spirit and that is when problems creep in. Eventually, no one will show for Monday Night Football and the party will be over. Don't introduce behaviors that are foreign to you in the beginning of a relationship. Most often, you won't be able to continue these patterns three to six months into the relationship, setting up a long pass down the field that will come up short and be incomplete.

Too many of these and you will be traded for another player. A wonderful and wise statement, made by my friend Jim Mullen, that I firmly believe in is, "Don't do anything in a relationship that you wouldn't do on a first date." Don't lose the ball to the other team - hold fast to those words of wisdom.

Winning the Heisman Trophy

You did your research, worked hard to be the best and received the Heisman Trophy for your efforts. Now the trophy sits in your showcase gathering dust. You may be doing the same thing with the woman in your life. If this is the case and you leave her in your showcase to gather dust, she will eventually dust herself off and scurry out of there. Just because you have won the trophy of her heart does not mean that the game is over. To win the game and to keep her heart, you must continue to date her throughout your entire relationship.

Fun Football Fact:
Who was the first paid professional football player and what is regarded as the birth date of professional football?

One time, when I was eleven and performing at a concert, I noticed an older couple dancing and laughing. They seemed to be totally in love based on my limited world of knowledge on the subject at the time. Because they intrigued me so much, after I finished performing, I went over to them and spent the next several hours talking to them about their relationship.

It turned out that they had been married for sixty-five years. After meeting and having an initial courtship of four days, they married. Yes that's right! Four days! (I am in no way encouraging anyone to get married after such a short length of time by any means. I am simply stating the facts.) They told me that they had been in love ever since and additionally had never been separated for more than a day or two during that period of time.

Upon asking them what their secret was, they told me that they laughed all the time, finding humor in the most mundane things; most importantly, though, they never lost the romance. When asked how they managed to sustain it after so much time, they said they always put each other first and continued to have a "date night" at least once a week, no matter what. With eight children and very little money, I couldn't fathom how they found the time or the money for just each other or could put each other first in most cases. They went on to say that they had never had any lengthy separations as previously stated; where one went, the other quickly followed. They also learned the correct way to disagree about things, sometimes just agreeing to disagree.

This last point was a new concept for me but proved to be an invaluable lesson. I learned that sometimes, no matter what we say or do, we simply cannot convince another person to come over to our point of view. In such a situation, it is much better to just shake hands and agree to disagree than end up in a heated no-win situation that builds up until it explodes without resolution.

As an eleven year old, I was learning a lot from this older couple. Yet, still I couldn't believe that they were able to be so touchy feely and so in love with each other after all those years. But this is how they looked to me as they spoke about their entire marriage. I dutifully went over to some of their family members who happened to be there, trying to disprove them.

I was happily surprised and suddenly hopeful about the reality of true love when the family members confirmed that they had always been like this and were truly in love. I was amazed by this couple and this encounter fueled my desire to learn more about relationships, how they work and why.

In football, even if you win all the games throughout the regular season and the playoffs, there is still the Super Bowl to be won. Even once you've arrived at the Super Bowl, if you haven't continued to work out and practice the plays, you may lose the biggest game of all. True romance is like the Super Bowl of relationships, the long and lasting one that may be a culmination of years of hard work and consistency. Once you "win" your partner over, the best way to let your marriage die is to stop practicing the plays that got you there in the first place. Allowing the everyday events of life to get in the way of your relationship will kill it, just as it would have if you had done that while you were first dating.

If you want to have a full and lasting marriage, one filled with strength, love and incredible sex, you will still have to do the work. The proof is in the pudding, so to speak, and the couple I mentioned above is not the only one that I have interviewed and observed over the years that were in love and had always been so even through the rough times. These observations have confirmed that romance can be kept alive if the right effort is put into it.

Jerry Morgan, a friend of mine, once told me, "Happy wife. Happy life." He is now eighty years old and happily in love with his best friend. In fact, they were childhood sweethearts! On the flip side of that, I think that the slogan could be changed too, "Busy life. Busy Wife." If you put everything else first in your life and only leave leftovers for your partner, this is a foul. Don't wait until the two-minute warning to get into the game; it may be too late!

Going back to the point of agreeing to disagree…today, while doing an interview on a national radio show, the host told me the following story, asking me what her best move should have been, and how to avoid bickering over little things in the future with her boyfriend. She and her boyfriend were going snowboarding one day with a bunch of friends. Her boyfriend proceeded to pack her vehicle with their snowboards, with the boards still hanging over the edge of the back of the car, not allowing the cargo door to be closed. She had previously packed the snowboards in her car on another occasion and knew if they were put in a certain way; the cargo door could be closed and suggested that to her boyfriend. An argument ensued, he wanting to leave the door open and she wanting to repack the snowboards so the door could be shut. This caused a small conundrum in their otherwise happy relationship.

I gave the following response to her question of how to handle this difference in opinion and the bickering that was caused when they couldn't agree on how to handle a problem. First I told her that in the future, she could just agree with him, then silently go back and repack the snowboards and shut the door.

However, I did tell her that this could cause some conflict as he may perceive that she doesn't trust his judgment. But if it bothered her greatly, as it seemed to do, then it might be one approach she could take. Then I told her something that threw her belief system about what the reason she perceived the argument to be about was, and that was the way the snowboards were packed, and made her see the entire situation in a completely different light.

I told her that most simple relational issues that resulted in bickering were actually caused by some underlying stress not neces- sarily having to do with the couple, but perhaps from outside sources. Since I did not know all of the circumstances, nor was her boyfriend there to give me his side of the conflicted situation, I would presume, from past encounters on this type of subject, that perhaps he was upset or stressed out about another situation entirely. I presented the idea that possibly he needed to have control in this one area to help validate his perception of his world at the time and additionally to help calm an internal conflict or stress he might be dealing with.

Revelation took over the tone of her voice, when she instantly stated that they had a bunch of family and friends who were staying with them during that week, and he had been very anxious and stressed out about it. Bingo! Immediately she understood his need for control in that situation and said that in the future she would try to look at the underlying causes of potential situations before she took control.

As I stated previously, he simply needed to have control over how the snowboards were packed, because internally he may have been feeling out of control in another other area of his personal or professional life. This is one of those times that it would have been best for their relationship for her to agree to disagree, and let him have his way. He would walk away happier, and less stressed about other matters if she had done so. Additionally, she would have scored a touchdown in the game of love that day.

Some things that seem so large, but are really very small, just don't matter in the grand scheme of things. It is better to let go of them and make your partner happy, then draw them out and have your own way, causing possible conflict and future dissent within the ranks of your team. *"So always do these things: Show mercy to others, be kind, humble, gentle and patient. Get along with each other, and forge each other...Do all these things; but most importantly, love each other. Love is what holds you all together in perfect unity. "* Colossians 3:12-14

The Thrill Is Gone

In relationships, generally speaking, the woman is the one who plays the role of nurturer more than the man. In the beginning, she treats you like a king and does everything she can to please you. She may make you breakfast in bed, leaves surprise notes on your car windshield, call you in the middle of the day just to whisper "I love you" and make other romantic gestures that let you know that she is thinking of you and that she loves you.

Later on, however, these little gestures stop. Sometimes it's because they get lost in the shuffle of life, other times it's due to bitterness in the relationship. When the gestures stop, discontent often follows. I have heard men make the following statements about their mates: "Where is the wife I married?" "She's not the same woman I first started dating. What's up with that?" "I just don't love her the same way anymore. She doesn't treat me like she did when we first got together!"

If you hear yourself making these statements or thinking along these lines, you need to look inside the relationship to see how far your romance has slipped. While most women love to give, if they consistently feel like they are being taken for granted and/or

Fun Football Fact:
William (Pudge) Heffelfinger was the first professional football player. The birth date of professional football is November 12, 1892. On that day, the Allegheny Athletic Association football team defeated the Pittsburgh Athletic Club (PAC). It was during that game that the PAC suspected that Heffelfinger, an AAA player, had been paid $500 for a game performance bonus.

While this practice was illegal at the time, there was no absolute proof that Pudge had been paid. The proof came eighty years later when the accounting records for the Allegheny Athletic Association were presented to the Pro Football Hall of Fame. This was the first incontrovertible proof of a player being paid to play the game. These records are commonly referred to as Pro Football's Birth Certificate.

feeling that the love and appreciation they have bestowed on you is not being reciprocated they will eventually start to do fewer and fewer of the things that they once loved to do for you. Sometimes, this occurs after they feel that they have tried to talk about their needs, but nothing has changed. Other times, it's because they're tired of giving and not getting anything back. In either case, the woman is grappling with the same question that you are: "Why doesn't he treat me the same way he did in the beginning?" So, they eventually give up.

If you wonder why her pampering has stopped and would like to get it back, you need to return to the way you treated her when you were first courting her. If you don't, she will never again treat you that way. Why should she?

Fun Football Fact:
What company makes the Vince Lombardi Super Bowl trophy?

As with football, if you don't give one hundred and ten percent to your team, eventually they will begin to resent you. Your teammates may know that you are making big bucks, but that you aren't showing up for practice and are taking credit for others' success. Eventually, either the coach will pull you out or your teammates will stop backing you up.

A woman will pull away from you if you don't hear her and you don't try to maintain the same attitude that you had towards her prior to your marriage. She will slowly stop giving to you and begin heading in a different direction, pulling a "reverse" that eventually gets you sacked.

To find out just how far you have let the romance in your relationship slip, ask yourself the following questions:

· Are you still behaving the same way with your partner that you did when you first started dating her?

· Are you still complimenting her?

· Do you make her feel like she is the only one in the room?

Fun Football Fact:
Tiffany and Company makes the Vince Lombardi Super Bowl trophy at a cost of $12,190.

· Are you still asking her questions, making her feel like you are interested in who she is and what she's thinking?

· Do you lovingly gaze at her and stroke her hair?

· Do you take her hand and hold it in yours when you walk?

· Do you still open doors for her?

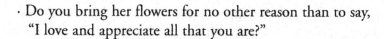

Fun Football Fact:
What quarterback holds the career record for being sacked the most times?

· Do you bring her flowers for no other reason than to say, "I love and appreciate all that you are?"

· Do you tell her "thank you" for the small kindnesses she bestows on you?

All of these things will go a long way towards restoring a happy and healthy relationship and can be considered the basics of romance. Don't stop courting her, just as a professional player would never stop practicing. Winners never quit.

Keeping the "Woo" in the Love Affair

Romance means "to have a love affair with; to woo. xvii" (The definition of "woo" is: "To seek the affection of with intent to romance. xviii") So how do you keep the love affair alive, and continue to "woo?" First, I think many people have a misconception of romance. When men hear a woman talk about romance and the lack of it in their relationship, many automatically assume that she means flowers, candlelit dinners, blue jewelry boxes from Tiffany's and long evenings spent gazing at the stars.

While all of these things are part of romance, there are other romantic actions and gestures that can be made apart from these. I often see men's necks bristle and tighten up when they hear their partner ask for a romantic evening. The media vision of romance is that of a couple going out on the town for the night.

Fun Football Fact:
John Elway holds the record for the most career sacks. He has been sacked 516 times!

The man shows up in his finest clothes and the woman descends from the staircase dressed to the nines. He hands her a beautiful bouquet of red roses and a box of chocolates and they proceed to the car, where he opens the door for her. He whisks her off to an enchanted evening, with a candlelit dinner at the finest restaurant in town followed by dancing and a lengthy walk on the beach as they share their most intimate thoughts.

Afterwards, they head to a cozy after-dinner establishment for more conversation and perhaps some cuddling. Just before they leave, the man hands the woman a box that holds a beautiful piece of jewelry that he has picked out just for her.

If that were a typical night of romance and I were a man, I would probably feel the same way- overwhelmed! Who could ever live up to that on a weekly basis? No one! Sure, it would be an awesome evening, but with all of that said, it's not realistic, nor is it often expected. With our busy lives, no one can plan an entire evening like that on a regular basis unless there's a huge staff behind them working out the details!

When most women speak of romance, they are speaking more about an emotional state of being and having a valuable bonding time with their loved one. If a woman says she would love a little romance, that is exactly what she means. This is one of the times, generally speaking, there are no hidden messages or meanings.

Romance, to a woman, can mean as little as holding her hand, gazing into her eyes and giving her a soft kiss. The point is to make time and room in your life for her. To keep your partner happy, you do need to have romance in your lives on a regular basis, meaning at least a few times a week. Women need romance to swell their emotions towards you. Maintaining romance will also vastly improve your sex life, as women tend to link romance with love and physical affection.

Let me give it to you straight, if the woman in your life says to you, "You're just like Novocain to me honey, because I'm not feeling you at all." You definitely need to get back into the romance game before you are permanently removed from her stadium.

Why is romance so important? One of the answers is that women are great multi-taskers. During the day, they will think of their partner many times. For example, a woman can be working on a plan for her company when her partner creeps into her thoughts.

Fun Football Fact:
Which NFL team has the record for the most consecutive games won?

She can be in the shower, at the gym, out to a business luncheon with a group of men or doing any other task and invariably her partner will be there in the recesses of her mind. Since most women think of their partner consistently throughout their day, they secretly hope that he is thinking about them as well. While this may be unrealistic, they still hold onto that hope. By being romantic, however, you can show the woman in your life that you have taken the time out of your day to think about her, no matter what else you have been doing.

It's not the flowers, cards or candy that hold so much value to a woman; it's the fact that you made the decision to think about her and then invested the time to make her feel special. Here are some examples of easy romantic things that you can do with your spouse that will help satisfy her need:

· Hold her hand and kiss her.

· Come up behind her, rub her shoulders and hold her. Most women love to be touched.

· Stroke her hair or touch her cheek while you are looking into her eyes during a conversation. That will send chills down her spine!

· When you are sitting on the couch talking, reach across and hold her hand. That single action will melt her and your conversation will become much more intimate and deep.

· When lying in bed, snuggle up behind her and whisper, "I love you," in her ear.

· Set up a bubble bath with candles for her and then join her in the tub.

· Offer to brush her hair and then lovingly do so.

· When talking with her, look directly in her eyes and then reach across and brush her neck with your lips before going back to your conversation. This will not only disarm her, but may lead to other things! Even so, sit back and DON'T expect anything more than that. This is not a move into the bedroom moment. It's just a brief moment that lets her know you find her attractive and helps pack romance in her emotional briefcase.

One day, while driving on a very narrow, unpaved and extremely dusty road, a friend of mine suddenly turned the car around and headed back in the opposite direction. At a certain point along the road, he again turned the car around, this time pulling over. Hopping out of the car, he bounded towards a cluster of sunflowers (he knew that they were my favorite flowers) and cutting one off, he brushed the bugs off and gave it to me. For the rest of the evening, he made sure that my sunflower was safe and had enough water to keep it fresh. That one, easy gesture will always stand out as one of the most romantic moments I have ever experienced and remains forever embedded in my heart and mind.

These are just a few examples of simple, yet romantic, gestures that will help recapture the heart of the woman in your life. Even so, this list does not excuse you from buying her flowers occasionally or taking her out for a memorable night on the town. Don't be passive in building or keeping your relationship strong and alive with romance and romantic gestures. Be proactive. Win the romance *game! "Let us not become weary in doing good, for at the proper time we will reap a harvest if we do not give up." Galatians 6:9*

Once you start reintroducing romance into your relationship, check your progress by asking her with sincerity if she feels that the relationship has improved. If she feels it hasn't, ask her what she thinks it would take to make improvements. But, whatever you do, don't shoot down her feelings by saying something like, "How can you think our relationship still has problems?"

If you make statements like that, she may not open up to you again for a long time. Rather, listen and be willing to hear what she is trying to say, even if you don't agree with it. While it may be hard for you to understand the emotions behind your partner's responses, she still feels them.

Fun Football Fact:
Until 2005, The Chicago Bears held the top two spots for the most consecutive games won: seventeen wins in the 1933-1934 season and sixteen in the 1941-1942 seasons! However, the New England Patriots broke that record during the 2004-2005 season with twenty-one consecutive games won!

In order to help you bridge the romance gap, look for the facts associated with her emotions. Once you find those facts, you will be able to better understand her needs and improve your relationship. Develop a plan to win the game.

For women, just because society sees the man as being the one who initiates romantic gestures, that does not leave you off the hook. You also need to take a proactive stance in the romance game as well as add spice in ways that he appreciates. If you don't know what romantic gestures would knock his socks off, ask him. For me, I often buy flowers for the men in my life. I can't tell you how many surprised looks and comments I have received over the years when I have done this. The most common response is, "No woman has ever brought me flowers before." A friend of mine with whom I once had a lunch meeting still comments, five years later, about the flowers that I brought him one day.

A Little Help in the Romance Game

Strategy is of the utmost importance when developing a winning football team. Organizing your strategy among all the players on the team is also key to optimizing your winning plays. The same holds true for romance.

You must have a strategy and organize it well in order to pull off the romance game. While the simple gestures I mentioned above are sure-fire ways to ignite the fire and feeling of romance for the woman in your life, these are just simple, basic exercises to get the ball moving towards the end zone. At least once a month, you should plan a truly romantic night out or a special getaway for you and your mate. This goes for both men and women. Perhaps you can even take turns doing this, alternating months. This is not your normal weekly date night, but a special night or weekend that is planned with great care and organization.

To plan that special night out and make it more than just the typical dinner and movie, you will need to learn about the different events and happenings that are in your area. See Chapter 15, *"Spending and Investing Time,"* as well as Chapter 17, *"The Last Pass,"* for ideas on ways to do this and places to go. Another good place to search for ideas is on the Internet. Using a search engine, put in key words or phrases such as: "what to do in - your city," "happenings - your city," "community calendar - your city," and so on. This should yield a whole crop of websites that list local events as well as other fun things to do that are special to your community.

If you have other couples that you are friends with, trade and share ideas on what to do. This will increase your database of knowledge. In any case, be creative. In the chapters noted above, I have listed a lot of really fun and creative ideas, for both freely spending and budget-conscious couples that are seeking a different approach than just the old staple of dinner and a movie.

CHAPTER 10
Learning the Playbook:
The Memory Game

Every player on the Carolina Panthers is issued a playbook when he joins the team. Inside that playbook are the team's plays, plans, strategies and terminology. Each player must commit everything within those pages to memory, which can be a daunting task, even for someone who has an excellent memory for details.

So how do the players accomplish this task? Above all, there has to be motivation; in this case, the motivating factors could be a paycheck, future career and the love of the game. But, motivation is only part of what will stimulate their memory cells to absorb the information they need to do their job.

Players must also use a variety of other methods, such as sight, sound and practical application in order to commit the playbook to memory. Such stimuli are very effective, even to those people who have the worst memories, and help foster association with information that needs to be recalled in the future.

Memory can be a powerful tool. A few days ago, I came across a car that was stranded in the middle of an intersection. There were a man and woman standing outside the car, with their backs to me. I slowed down to ask if they needed assistance. When the woman turned my way, she looked at me and instantly called out my name, running over to take my hand. I was shocked!

I hadn't seen her since my childhood, yet she remembered my name! She even remembered various attributes about me. When we were kids, she was in the popular group of kids and I was not, but she always made time for everyone and did not differentiate between those who had money and those who did not (I did remember that much!).

Fun Football Fact:
Who was the first running back to make the NFL record books for holding the team records for most yards rushed on three different teams?

Fun Football Fact:
The first running back in the NFL record books with the most yards rushed for three different teams is Ricky Watters with 1,000 yards!

I was embarrassed, because while she had remembered my name instantly, I wasn't certain of hers. The big question on my mind for the rest of that day was how she had remembered my name so easily! Since I was a child, I have been involved in theater. There have been many times that I have been asked to fill in for lead roles at the last minute, sometimes memorizing as many as two hundred pages of script in as little as a few hours. And yet, why do I have a hard time remembering names and birthdays?

After that incident, I had my motivation to find out why. The first theory I came up with before I researched the subject matter was that names and dates don't necessarily have an emotional impact unless they are associated with something that affects us in a more than simple way. I thought perhaps an emotional word picture might help me win the memory game. In any case, I didn't want to be embarrassed if this ever happened again, so I started to research human memory and ways to improve it. The answer that I found was a simple one and can help anyone who really gives it a try.

The answer lies in creating word association or mnemonics, a formula or rhyme that helps you remember names, birthdays, order lists, etc. Using these methods along with the techniques I explained to you about emotional word pictures previously, can help even those of us with the worst memories improve our retention. While some people have amazing memories, many, like me, do not. For those of us who were not born with the inherent ability to memorize facts, dates and names through a natural association, however, there is hope.

Memory is the ability to retain and recall past experiences or information. Scientific studies show that this act probably takes place in many areas of the brain. [xix] The most specific areas of the brain to which science has been able to assign a link to memory are the limbic system (which is located near the center of the brain and controls mood and attitude) and the temporal lobes (which are located near the base of the skull and deal with memory and experience). While scientific data is deficient in defining the exact causes and placement of memory, years of research have revealed how the process goes through the stages of recording, retaining and recall. Doing this, the brain records information from the sensory organs and brings that information to the short-term memory.

Research studies show that short-term memory only takes in a certain amount of information at a time before it begins to dump older, less relevant information. A person's ability to record, retain and recall information can be improved with practice, but will also be limited by the extent of their basic attention span. Short-term memory is used mostly for trivial information, while long-term memory is generally reserved for more important information. Your brain determines which memory bank to use in each case, depending on how you have indexed your words, but more importantly the values you have acquired throughout your life. While you may be able to record and retain information easily on a mostly subconscious level, recalling information is much more complex.

To recall information with more ease, you need to use some sort of an association or go back to the moment in which you first recorded the information. In conducting my research, I've found that scientists and research analysts who deal with memory and its attributes all say the same thing: association has been proven to be an extremely effective tool in remembering data.

For example, if you're in the garage, you may make a list in your head of the things you need to do once you finish the project you're working on. Later, once inside the house, you may recall that you had made the list but now you have forgotten what was on the list. To help you recall, go back to the moment in which you made the list by walking back into the garage and retracing your steps. Suddenly, you remember. That's association. By going back to the point of origin, you associated the garage with the list you had made in your head. Once you were back in the garage, the list came to the forefront of your memory, out of the subconscious and into the conscious recall memory banks.

However, this is just one technique and not always a feasible way to remember things. What if you had made a list while you were walking down the entryway to board a plane? It would be impossible to go back to that moment without a lot of time and money. So what would you do?

There are other ways to make associations with the lists that are locked away in your memory banks, not the least of which is when you are in a situation that cannot be easily retraced in the future, such as the one above. In these cases, try to associate your list with something more tangible and easily accessible.

One way to remember something is to associate it with another item that has a particular feeling (remember feeling commits things to memory) or special meaning for you. Russell Crowe did this perfectly when he got married on his birthday.

Since his birthday already had a special meaning to him (not that his marriage doesn't) and has been with him his entire life, by aligning his future wedding anniversaries with a very personal event in his life, his birthday, he will always remember his anniversary. Sheer genius! I don't foresee him having any hurt feelings over a missed anniversary.

As I pointed out before, I have a hard time remembering names, so how can I help my memory in that area? First, I must simply admit that I have a hard time in that area and give myself a bit of leeway. Second, I must become proactive and start a new pattern that helps me overcome this area of weakness. How? By association or mnemonics.

Fun Football Fact:
Who holds the record for the most rushing attempts in a career?

Here is an example of using such a strategy. Suppose I meet a man whose name is Gerald Cunnings on a rainy day in New York City. A few years later, I bump into him at a supermarket in Buffalo, but I haven't seen him since our sole meeting a few years ago. How do I help myself remember his name? I would need to make an effort to remember Gerald Cunnings' name in case I ran into him again in the future. He would then feel important that I could rattle his name off much like my friend had made me feel so by effortlessly recalling my name along the roadside.

The key is to use a number of tactics when you first meet a person. For example, when I first meet Gerald, I need to associate his name with something familiar. Since it is a rainy day, I can use that. "Cunnings" makes me think of the word "sunning" (okay, not a common word, but used occasionally when "sunning" yourself). So, I could make up a rhyme, such as, "It was a rainy day when I met Gerald Cunnings, no sunning myself today." Doing so, I have now associated his last name, Cunnings, with the lack of sun. Gerald rhymes with Herald, so I can say to myself, "Gerald wasn't in the Miami Herald because it was raining in New York, but sunny in Florida."

I have now associated his first and last names with specific events that have meaning to me. I have successfully used the linking and rhythmic method of a mnemonic device to help me remember. Additionally, when I first meet Gerald, I should take his hand in mine and shake it, adding the sense of touch to my memory cell. Also, during our initial conversation, I need to use his name several times while looking him in the eyes to help engrain it in my brain. Finally, once I walk away from him, I need to review his name in my mind and recall whatever part of his face or body that I found to be unique to his name. Perhaps I can create an emotional word picture at that time to help me. All of these simple techniques help my memory cells develop an association between his face and name.

If someone has an unusual name, you can also ask that person how it's spelt and what the origin is. Let me use the name "Tatianna" as an example. If I were to meet a woman named Tatianna, I might ask her what country of origin her name is and whether there's any special family history associated with it.

If she tells me a story about her name, it's highly likely that I will remember it. Stories create an emotional link between the word and the brain. In this case, I may find out that Tatianna is of Russian origin and its English translation would be Tonya.

Association takes practice, and while the above examples may seem silly to you, they do work. The next challenge for me, however, was to remember birthdays without any outside reminders. While I have a memory pocket book that enables me to write birthday cards ahead of time and have them ready each month, and an IPAQ (hey, I need all the help I can get!), I wanted to be able to remember special dates on my own.

Remembering birthdays by association was a lot harder for me, but also extremely important. A birthday, being the celebration of the day someone was born, reminds me that had that person not been born, they wouldn't be able to enrich my life. Therefore, it's very important to me that I remember and celebrate the birthdays of those close to me. So how can I associate birthdays? Let's say that my boyfriend's birthday is on April 19 and I want to make sure that I never forget it.

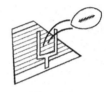

Fun Football Fact:
Walter Payton holds the record for the most rushing attempts. He has carried the ball nearly 4000 times!

April is a spring month and a good time to begin planting a garden. Therefore, the first thing I can do is associate my boyfriend's birthday with a sunflower because they are happy flowers to me and his birthday is in a month in which I would plant them. Just as they smile, my boyfriend usually brings a smile to my face.

While associating the month is not as difficult, however, the number is a little bit harder for me. There aren't a great deal of things that I can associate with a number, so I have to make up something that will still have meaning. In the case of my boyfriend's birthday, I could use the phrase "I planted nineteen rows of sunflowers in my garden in April." Now, I have successfully made an association. While this seems like a lengthy process at first, you will get better at it the more you practice and the time it takes for you to commit something to memory will become shorter and shorter. Your association doesn't have to be a complicated one; it can be as simple as a picture that puts the two pieces of information together (linking). If you are creative with your associations, your memory will improve greatly.

When it comes to our special dates, birthdays and anniversaries, we all feel the same way. We say things like, "But it's the same date every year. It never changes. Why can't he/she remember?" What we all need to understand is that it's not a personal thing when a loved one forgets a special date. However, those of us who are poor at remembering dates can make the decision to either change and improve our memory or get a special calendar book like the one I mentioned earlier.

Those who are affected by our poor memories can help us by encouraging us with sweet reminders. It may take years of training or perhaps even a lifetime of working with you partner to see progress, but reminders will ultimately help. If you want your partner to remember special dates, make notes on a big calendar. For example, put a heart around the month of February and circle the 14th with another large red heart. Try doing the same for your anniversary and your birthday.

Start reminding your partner gently at the beginning of that month. This will take away the frustration surrounding the event for both of you. Whatever you do, don't nag or use negative remarks such as, "I'm sure you won't remember. You never do." If you do so, you are setting them up for failure and they may ultimately never feel like they can please you. It follows that if they feel like they can never please you, then they will wonder why they should even bother.

As a little side note, using one's poor memory as an excuse for everything soon gets old and becomes inexcusable. Every year, you know when the first game of the NFL season and when the Super Bowl are. Even though the days and dates change from year to year, you make special plans for those days. The same process that you used to memorize those dates and make a point of celebrating them in whatever fashion, can be used to remember birthdays, anniversaries and other occasions that happen on the same day every year.

Fun Football Fact:
When was the first NFL game?

CHAPTER 11
The Team—True Intimacy, the Road to Becoming Better Friends

Coaches and players on a football team spend a lot of time together both on the road and on the field. During that time, they become more intimately involved in each other's lives. They can't help but know when someone is about to have a baby, what one another's favorite foods are, who broke what bone on the field or what annoys other members of their team.

Creating such closeness helps to develop a bond that fosters trust and respect for each other both on and off the field. However, that trust and respect is not earned overnight. It takes time, patience, the occasional swallowing of pride, forgiveness and communication to really create the intimacy required for a functional winning team.

The same is true of any relationship, whether it's on or off the field. Men and women around the world are ravenous for true intimacy in their relationships but can't seem to incorporate it into their daily lives. We all desire intimacy and want a partner who can also be our best friend, but divorce statistics are proving that this is not what is happening within our relationships.

With the National Center for Health Statistics indicating that 40% of marriages in the United States alone are ending in divorce, what can we do to beat the odds? How can we stop the demise of marriage and prevent the silent death that envelops so many couples? One of the main reasons for this breakdown of true intimacy is something that has been said over and over again: men and women don't speak the same language or have the same ways of accessing information, creating a communication gap that eventually destroys relationships.

Just because men and women aren't always in the same area code in terms of how they understand each others language and the depth of intimacy each requires to build a solid relationship, does NOT mean they can't dial the same number to get there.

Let me start at the beginning of a relationship and look at what draws men and women together at that first moment. As a general rule, men are visual and tactilely motivated. They are initially looking for physical bonding. Women are generally auditory, motivated by emotion and initially looking for emotional bonding.

Fun Football Fact:
On October 3, 1920 the first NFL games were played. Both games were shut out games. The teams? The Dayton Triangles vs. the Columbus Panhandles 14 - 0 and the Rock Island Independents vs. the Muncie Flyers 45 - 0.

When a man sees a woman that he perceives as beautiful walk into a room, it will visually stimulate him. He may look at her and map out a plan to start up a conversation. His heart may begin to beat faster as he approaches her, ready to fulfill his desire for contact. If he is able to make contact with her, figuratively speaking, and they go out on their first date, he will wonder invariably how to get to the first touch. Whether it's as simple as holding her hand or putting an arm around her waist, or aiming for a more intimate kiss, he will spend more time during the date trying to figure out a way to get to that tactile moment than trying to build an emotional bond. Most men do want emotional intimacy, but many equate that intimacy with the physical realm. The visual and tactile part of a man's being needs to be satisfied before any true emotional bond can form for him. Opposingly, when a woman sees a man that intrigues her walk into a room, he may visually stimulate her but she is not necessarily drawn enough to walk over and speak with him.

A woman is more likely to want to find out who he is, what he does and how he thinks before she develops any real interest in him. If she decides to go on a date with him, she will think more about what his values are than how to achieve physical contact.

Women love physical contact, but it's more important for them to find out how a man treats his mother, what his family life was like, his value system and what his emotional history is. Most women do not equate intimacy with physical contact. Rather, physical intimacy, to most women, is a result of emotional intimacy.

Emotional intimacy is the motivating factor for a woman's true desire for physical contact. A woman won't necessarily want to proceed to the tactile stage until she finds out the vital statistics of how a man thinks and behaves. How she perceives him as a person will directly affect whether or not she wants to proceed any further in the relationship. (The motivational factors listed above for men and women achieving emotional intimacy are based on the general population only, some men and women do not fall into this box.)

While women tend to need an emotional connection to validate their relationships, men tend to need physical contact to verify theirs. Men need that tactile moment that will break the emotional barrier for them, perhaps a throwback to their childhood. Growing up, many men don't experience a lot of physical contact, such as hugging, touching or holding hands with the people around them because these are not "manly" things to do. Once they reach a certain age, they are trained to believe that the only acceptable physical contact between people is that between two people in a relationship.

Women, by contrast, are in constant contact with others, both during their childhood and in their adult lives. Hugging, touching, and holding hands or putting an arm around the waist of a friend are all accepted means of nonverbal communication between two females. No one looks at them differently, whether they are children or adults. Many men would not feel comfortable with the same level of physical contact unless they were in a relationship, believing that they would be looked upon differently if they were to behave in this manner as an adult.

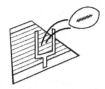

Fun Football Fact:
When was the first Super Bowl played?

Here is a classic example of the differences in something deemed "acceptable" for women, but "unacceptable" for men. My friends and I, to date, still have slumber parties. Not quite like the ones we had as children, but similar. The girls get together, without their husbands or boyfriends, and watch Anne of Green Gables or some other appropriate "chick flick," pig out, and laugh all night. One of my dearest friends' mothers still has slumber parties with her best friend from childhood. While having a slumber party for a woman is an acceptable form of bonding, if a man were to tell his male friends that he was having a slumber party and invite them over to join in the fun, he would be looked upon strangely, and quite possibly ignored in the future or given an intervention party by well meaning friends. Get the picture?

While I firmly believe that both men and women really do need the same amount of physical contact, I also believe that men are generally deprived in this area. Couple the lack of physical contact in a man's formative years with their basic genetic coding as "left-brain" individuals and you have a clearer picture as to why emotional intimacy will not necessarily be an instinctual part of a man's make-up. Even though emotional intimacy may not be instinctual to the general male population, it can become a learned response. If you are a visual person it may be hard to change your initial reaction to external stimuli, but you can make the decision to become a seeker of emotional intimacy before you dive into the physical realm. That is one of the greatest attributes of a "left-brain" individual. You are excellent at making decisions. While you will always be motivated by visual stimulation, you can learn to develop an emotional bond before you have physical contact with a woman. There is no magic potion or secret knowledge that can do this for you. Instead, you need to make the decision to incorporate a new routine into your make-up, one that will take practice and discipline, but is achievable and eventually will become very enjoyable.

Of course, these are generalizations and there are men and women who do not fit into these roles, but if we are honest with ourselves, without trying to impress the opposite sex in what we want them to believe about us, these are the facts.

Achieving Emotional Intimacy

Fun Football Fact:
The first Super Bowl was played on January 15, 1967. The Green Bay Packers defeated the Kansas City Chiefs 35 - 10!

One of the first steps to achieving emotional intimacy is to honor the woman in your life. That is, you must maintain a "high respect or esteem. [xx]" for her. Your relationship will be mutually fulfilling if you do so. But, how do you actually honor her? You can honor the woman in your life in a number of ways. For example, you can simply start off with a little gesture like opening the door for her. This could lead to bigger things, like taking an interest in her entire family and treating her and her family with respect and admiration.

When you begin to honor her, your intimacy level will go up. She will perceive it as nurturing and loving care for her. The definition of "nurture" is, "To nourish; feed. To foster; cultivate. [xxi]" When you nurture your partner, you are nourishing or feeding their soul. You are cultivating intimacy. Here is a list of a few ways that you can honor your loved one to help cultivate deeper intimacy in your relationship:

· Help her parents with a project.

· Get a Mother's or Father's Day card for both of her parents.

· Go to her softball game or other activity to cheer her on. (She goes to yours after all!)

· Open the door for her.

· Pull a chair out for her.

· Stay in bed with your spouse in the morning, gently running your hands across her body and watch her as she wakes up. (This will send a message that you find her very attractive. You will go all the way to the end zone with that maneuver! It's very sexy!)

· Tell others about all the wonderful attributes you find in her, both while she is around and when she is not.

· Help her put her coat on.

· Surprise her by cleaning the bathroom without any outside prompting.

· Most importantly, have meaningful conversations with her - ask her deep questions. Examples would be: Asking her more about her childhood dreams and the hopes and dreams she has for the future. Or ask her about one thing that impressed her most that particular day.

These are all easy questions that do not require you to even answer or act on, only to listen to. But it will do wonders to help build your intimacy level with her if you ask her these questions from time to time. As I mentioned before, men tend to derive intimacy from physical contact. It helps build a sense of bonding for them and helps to stimulate the production of Oxytocin in their body (more on that later). It also helps the male feel attractive. In this same way, words and emotional bonding create those feelings in a female.

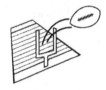

Fun Football Fact: How did the New England Patriots receive their name?

These are just a few simple things that will show her that you are honoring her. I'm sure you can come up with many more on your own. When you honor her in these ways, you will make her feel special and she will feel like she is a valuable part of your life.

As I wrote before, women think of their partner fairly consistently throughout their day, while men tend to only think of the task or situation at hand. Men tend to compartmentalize, which is the way they are wired and what makes them so unique and gifted in their special way.

When you honor your partner, you give her the illusion that you are thinking of her as often as she thinks of you. This is extremely fulfilling to a woman and helps her to feel valued and appreciated. When you don't honor your partner, however, you are lowering the value you place on her. If that happens, it will also lower her sense of self-esteem. To combat this, she may try to provoke feelings of value in other ways or get validation from other sources.

If a woman does not feel that she is honored or valued at home, she may look for a relationship outside her present one to fill the gap, thus creating a "substitution" mid-game. Because women are capable of having platonic relationships with men, she may initially seek a male "substitute" to fill that gap. However, as she becomes more emotionally bonded with him, she may develop a deeper friendship than the one she had originally intended. If she must turn to someone else to meet her basic needs, danger is brewing. You have just allowed a "trap block" to occur in your relationship, but the outcome won't be under your control and you may not get a chance to tackle the opposing team member to keep him from getting through to the end zone.

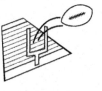

Fun Football Fact:
The New England Patriots received their name because the area they reside in is the birthplace of the American Revolution.

Just as a football team will look for a player to replace you if you aren't fulfilling your role, a woman will draft another player into your position if you aren't meeting her basic needs in the relationship. As she begins spending more time with other people and making less time for you, while your mate may not necessarily be seeking to replace you, it can lead to problems if the behavior continues. Your football team begins with great expectations for you as their star quarterback. However, if you don't make consistent passes, put real effort into the game or run the ball consistently without communicating with your coach and teammates, you may end up temporarily benched, or even worse, cut entirely from the team roster.

Much the same is true of a relationship of any kind. If it's important to you, you will make the time and put the effort in to honor it. You can turn your relationship around in a short period of time when you honor your partner and keep the lines of communication open with her. The trick is to be consistent. Believe it or not, you have the power to cause the most secure and drop-dead gorgeous woman in the world to begin to have feelings of insecurity and inadequacy when you don't value her. The result of devaluing the woman in your life can have devastating penalties. Are you willing and ready to pay the price? Emotional intimacy can be harder for a man for a number of reasons, including the way he was raised (as stated previously), as well as inherent insecurities. But, if you want a woman who treats you better than you could have imagined in your wildest dreams, you need to block the defensive line. If this is a really tough issue for you, you may want to talk to a side or line judge and seek professional counseling or a support group that deals with these issues; this can be very cathartic for you.

If you don't resolve this issue, you can never have a truly fulfilling relationship. You will spend your life going from one relationship to the next, always searching for something you thought was missing in the previous relationship. What you haven't realized yet is that you are looking for emotional intimacy to perhaps fill the need you did not get when you were growing up.

Fun Football Fact: When did the NFL use the penalty flag for the first time?

My friend Barbara once gave me a good example of how the different sexes build relationships and create intimacy. She created the following analogy: If you took two women and two men and had the women go shopping for the day and the men fishing on a boat, the women would come back the best of friends, knowing the intimate details of each other's lives and families. The men, by contrast, would come back from their day of fishing only knowing how many fish each of them had caught.

A good point to remember from this part of the book is that women are looking for relational bonding while men are seeking facts. I am not implying that men are shallow, only that they are coded differently.

Better Friendships

If you want to have a deeper, more intimate relationship, become her best friend. There are several steps you can take to learn to be a better friend to your partner. Include her in the things you love to do. This will foster emotional bonding and will make her feel that she is important enough in your life to share in the things that you love to do.

Touch her in non-sexual ways: caress her arm, rub her shoulders, hold her hand or place your hand on the small of her back and keep it there. Ask her opinion on things that are important to you. Have a conversation about life, friendship, family or politics (assuming that you are on the same page as she is; otherwise, steer clear of these waters if your relationship is not on stable ground).

These are just a few of the things that you can do to deepen your friendship with her. In addition, you should read books and study other relationships to find ways to become more open about your feelings. Women tend to have deeper relationships than men do because they aren't criticized by society for being open and vulnerable. Stop hiding behind the fear that you won't be accepted for who you are or that you will be judged by outside entities; go beyond your comfort zone. Start learning to disclose who you are and what you are thinking. The more you are able to reveal your vulnerabilities to her, the more comfortable she will feel with you. If you can master this, you will experience a freedom in your life that you never dreamt was possible. Here's a simple list of things that will help cultivate your friendship:

- Be kind. Simple, I know, but very profound.

- Be liberal with sincere compliments. Don't withhold your love because you are in a bad mood. That's a holding foul and is accompanied by a penalty flag and a ten-yard penalty!

- Talk to her. Communication is the main ingredient in a deep relationship. Without it, she may begin to feel left out and lonely. Neither sex can read minds, so verbal communication is the key.

- Learn to listen without judging and ask questions that invoke an answer. "What did you think about that situation?" "How did that affect what you thought about the outcome?" *"It is love that asks, that seeks, that knocks, that finds, and that is faithful to what it finds." St. Augustine.*

- One of the most important things that friends do is laugh together. Laughter is one of the main ingredients to all of the healthy and happy relationships that I have known over the years. Why do you think many comics live longer than the average population? Because true comics are generally happy people. George Burns is a great example of this and Bob Hope is another. In the same way, couples who truly laugh together are generally the happiest couples.

- Don't bring up past wrongs. Let go of what's gone and move on from this day forward. This especially holds true for any thing that is in the past of your loved one. Never use some thing they have lovingly entrusted you with about themselves against them in the future, especially if you are in a heated argument. You knew they had a past when you became involved with them and it had nothing to do with you or your future. (This is not to say you should not research their past behaviors and history. I am strictly talking about past mistakes or bad decisions they may have made in their past that do not directly affect your relationship in the present or future.) *"Brethren, I do not consider that I have made it my own; but one thing I do, forgetting what lies behind and straining forward to what lies ahead." Philippians 4:13*

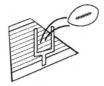

· Don't ignore even the smallest problems that may arise; just because the storm settles doesn't mean that the wind will blow it away. Meaning, just because you forget, doesn't mean that your partner will also. Problems are insidious things that seep into every area of a relationship if they are not brought out into the open and resolved. A problem left unresolved will compound and fester, eventually causing a gaping wound. If you let it get that far, invariably infection will set in. Once infection sets into your relationship, the woman in your life may chop off the offending limb, namely you, and discard it. Resolve your problems now!

Fun Football Fact:
The NFL used the penalty flag for the first time on September 17, 1948. It was used during a Green Bay Packers vs. Boston Yanks game.

· Don't take the anger of your day out on the loved ones around you. *"Better a patient man than a warrior, a man who controls his temper than one who takes a city." Proverbs 16:32*

· Forgive. Make a commitment to your partner to never go to bed angry. Achieve some measure of resolution before your head hits the pillows. *"Be angry, but do not sin; do not let the sun go down on your anger." Ephesians 4:26*

· Make a commitment to say "I love you" every day and every night, even when you don't "feel" it. Love is a gift, NOT a right. It's a decision and a commitment, not a feeling. The feeling you feel when you are in the first flush of "love," is the chemical reaction better known as attraction or "falling in love." If you can fall in love, you can fall out of it just as well.

· Never put conditions on your partner; love is not a conditional thing. For example, don't say things like, "If you just did (blank), I would find you more attractive." Or "Well, you've gained weight and I just can't touch you looking that way." Negative statements like these, especially the latter one, will discourage your partner and make them feel very insecure. This "unsportsmanlike conduct" will cause more weight gain or other negative unintended effects including losing the ball. Instead, encourage your partner without talking about his or her weight and make the decision to kiss and hold them. If your partner has a weight problem, start taking walks with him or her, thereby having the added effect of building your relationship while exercising. By doing so, you are adding value to your partner and building up their self-esteem meter. Since the weight gain is only a symptom of a deeper problem, you need to focus on treating that problem before the symptom will go away.

Above all, invest time to cultivate your friendship. No matter how busy your schedule, there is always a way to make room for someone who is important to you. If your relationship is important to you, you must make time. Just as a football player runs the extra miles, takes extra classes and spends the wee hours of the morning to read and learn more about his game in order to impress his coach, team and hone his skills to become a better player, so too, you must practice the same disciplines for your relationship.

Women: Compliment your partner and notice when he does even the smallest positive deed. That will encourage him to rise up and do more. It makes him feel like you believe in him, which you should! When you expect the best from people, you will usually get it. Men are as sensitive to praise and encouragement as women are.

Also, don't nitpick when he does things. If he cleans the toilet, don't criticize the way he did it if he didn't do it the way you would. Of course he didn't do it your way because he's not you! Rather, be happy that he did it at all.

When I was nine years old, a neighbor hired me to wash his windows. I desperately needed a winter jacket and the twenty dollars he was going to pay me to do all of the windows in his house would go a long way to purchase one for me for the upcoming winter months. To begin with, he assigned the sliding glass doors at the back of the house for me to work on. I worked very hard to achieve the result of the spotless shinny glass, which he wanted. However, each time I finished one of the doors, he would come over and find a small streak on one of them and tell me to wash it again.

After what seemed like an entire summer day of washing just that one sliding glass door in every way he showed me, he still told me it was done inadequately and was not clean enough for him. Finally I left, knowing that no matter how hard I worked or how clean the door was, it would never be up to his standards. He never paid me for the sliding glass door that took several hours and it left a deep impression on me about failure and the inability to please someone. When you criticize someone continually for something they have worked hard on in order to please you, you are crushing their spirit and causing them to stop wanting to continue working on whatever you criticized them about. This particular subject was highly commented on during the survey I took of men. So watch and be aware of your comments women, because you are discouraging the men in your life, just as my neighbor did to me.

Men: I have heard a lot of men say to their partners, "It's never good enough anyway, so why bother?" Don't use that poor excuse to avoid helping around the house or with other tasks.

Making Time

Making time for your relationship is very important; in fact, it's paramount. I know I keep stating this in a variety of ways, but I can't stress that point enough. When I have spoken to people who have made their lives very busy, generally speaking, the relationships they are in are deteriorating fast and they don't know what to do. (No one can "make" your life busy. You are the one who ultimately makes the final choices in your life.)

I hear these people say the same thing over and over again in a variety of ways, "I just don't have enough time to invest in the relationship and now he/she is complaining. I don't know what to do." Meanwhile, they are standing there talking to me when they could be investing that "time" with the person who is complaining!

Let me give you a few examples of "lost time" in case you are the one who always believes you don't have "the time." Do you ever sit down to read a book, watch television, read the newspaper or speak with someone on the phone while not at work? If so, then you have successfully made time for each of these activities outside of your relationship. That is all time you have made for things that are not as important as the loved ones around you. If you have time for those activities, you certainly have time for your partner. It's all a matter of priority. If you are making time for everything else, but not your partner, then you are shouting loud and clear what your priorities are and what they are not. While there are some things in life that do cause our lives to become excessively busy at times, often it's a matter of reorganizing our activities differently in order to allow more time for those we hold dear.

Most people need a little "down time" or "personal time" to engage in activities that are strictly for themselves such as reading, talking with friends, writing, etc. That down time is perfectly acceptable and expected in any relationship. However, in most of the "busy life" masses (and I use that particular word deliberately because it's becoming an epidemic in our society) that I have spoken too, after further investigation into their lives, have quite a bit of "me" time. If you have too much "me" time, you will be pushing the "us" out of the "relationship" or "team" equation and may end up fumbling the ball five yards shy of the end zone.

So how do you change such a pattern? First, you will really have to make a conscious effort. Everyone walking the Earth has most likely fallen victim to the "I just don't have time" syndrome at some time or another. So what do you do? To begin with, start a weekly ritual and stay committed to it! A ritual will draw both of you closer together.

It's time out just for the two of you, no matter what else may seem to get in the way. If your relationship is not ready for a date night, start out by making just ten minutes every other day and then work up to sixty minutes one time a week of just "your" time together to begin heading in the right direction.

Fun Football Fact:
When did NFL officials replace the collegiate rules and adopt rules expressly for the NFL?

Once you have established this minor time as part of your regular routine, begin working toward a full date night. All of the couples in successful marriages that I have spoken with say the same thing: Have a date night and don't break it no matter what! Even if you have children and the babysitter is ill, put the kids to bed early and have a date at home. Saying "no" to everyone and everything else and "yes" to each other on that night will build a strong and lasting relationship.

Remember, don't ever let your ritual go, even if you have been married for seventy-three years and don't feel like participating in it any longer. If you keep committed to your rituals, the rewards will be endless. In fact, I've heard many couples say that sex in their seventies and eighties is alive and well. But, remember that you may get a "no nookie for you cookie" if you haven't done the work to keep that romance alive!

CHAPTER 12
Recruiting and Stats—Things Women Need You to Know

When the Chicago Bears are recruiting top players for their team, they base their decisions on a player's statistics and determine how much they are willing to pay for the contract of that player. When you choose a woman, you are essentially recruiting her based on her stats.

A woman's "stats" may be derived from such criteria as her appearance, body type, sense of humor, background and education, to name just a few. This process is similar for women as they choose men. Below is a poll taken from women of all ages and backgrounds on what they look for in the "stats" of men as well as what turns them off. The results of this survey are based on interviews with three hundred women randomly selected over the course of a year and a half. While there are a few additional "stats" that I would add to my personal list, this is a poll, and remains unbiased.

The Almost Perfect Mate

· A man who is hygienically clean and well-groomed.

· A man who is confident in himself and comfortable in his skin.

· A man who is financially stable.

· A man who has a good sense of humor.

· A man who is intelligent.

· A man who is well-mannered. (E.g. opens doors, introduces you to his family and friends, not crass, etc.)

· A man who is physically fit and healthy.

· A man who is a good listener, interested in who their partner is and what she has to say.

· A man who is conscientious and patient about her needs in bed.

· A man who follows through on verbal commitments.

The "Don't Go There Ever" Man

· A man who does not follow through on commitments.

· A man who is conceited or arrogant.

· A man who behaves in a lewd or lascivious manner. Pornography and strip clubs do not appeal to the majority of women. They may quietly put up with it, pretending that it's okay and even joining in his "fun," but they secretly resent him for it. This resentment will rear its ugly head eventually. On this point, 89% of the women polled agreed. Believe it! When I asked why, if they secretly resented the men, they still participated instead of speaking up, they said that they wanted to please the man in their life. However, most said eventually that it progressively turned them off and they lost interest sexually as this type of behavior continued.

· A man who is hygienically challenged. (Brush your tongue because it holds an immense amount of bacteria and odor!)

· A man who smokes or drinks heavily.

· A man who uses the toilet brush technique when kissing his partner. (see below)

· A man who plays emotional games.

· And, finally, one of the biggest turn off's? A man who dates several women at once. I have heard men call it, "serial dating." This instantly signals to a woman that the man lacks self-confidence and needs constant assurance. Even more importantly, this type of man probably would never be monogamous or trustworthy, basically remaining insecure and continuing his pattern of behavior even in a "committed" relationship.

In presenting this information, I am just stating the facts of the poll conducted; I am NOT making judgments. In my original book, I left out some of this data, but, because I thought that it was important enough to inform men about what women really think, I've included it in this version. Continued polling has shown it to be overwhelming in evidence. As I said earlier, this book, while geared for men, is also important for women. So women…don't feel left out here. I also conducted a survey of a little over one hundred men, here is what they had to say about women and the "stats" that they find important!

The Almost Perfect Female

· A woman who takes care of her body.

· A woman who is secure in who she is.

· A woman who has a stable career, not just a job.

· A woman who is clean.

· A woman who has it together emotionally.

· A woman who has her own set of friends and doesn't need to always be with a man.

The "Don't Go There Ever" Woman

· A woman who doesn't take care of herself or doesn't take pride in her appearance.

· A woman who is hygienically challenged.

· A woman who is clingy.

· A woman who is emotionally needy.

· A woman who is gossipy.

· A woman who doesn't support her man; a naggy woman.

· A woman who sleeps around.

· A woman who plays head games.

· A woman who doesn't know what she wants and can't make up her mind.

· A woman who is financially needy.

Fun Football Fact:
On February 25, 1933, NFL officials replaced the collegiate rules and adopted rules expressly for the NFL.

Here are a few additional things you need to know about women before you begin recruiting.

· When a woman asks if she can talk to you, don't assume it's because she wants to attack you or solve a relationship issue. Most often, she simply wants to sit with you, spend time and talk casually. To avoid a "false start," and if you aren't sure of her directive, ask. If you go on the offensive, she will go on the defensive. That is a tactical error and may cost you your turn with the ball. Women hate it when men say, "a man will be a man." It's a poor excuse to hide behind.

· Don't emotionally starve a woman or you'll be in emotional debt. Too much debt and you will end up in bankruptcy court! Emotionally bankruptcy is a death sentence for a relationship. When athletes train for a game, they work their muscles to make them strong, fast and flexible. If the athlete doesn't train his muscles, they will atrophy. The same holds true with a relationship. Emotional starvation will cause your relationship to atrophy.

· Women won't be your "beck-and-call girls." Plan ahead. Don't consistently call at the last minute and expect her to drop everything for you. While spontaneity is fun occasionally, resentment will grow if this is the only way she can invest time with you. Make sure to have a "ready list" made to use for date night.

· Scoring with women in the bedroom is like making a long drive down the field for a touchdown; they are relationship-oriented regarding sex. If you don't follow the plays, you will have an incomplete pass and lose possession of the ball. Men are more like field goals when it comes to sex. If a woman kicks the ball, she's sure to make it to the end zone. Whether or not she scores 1, 2, or 3 points, will depend on her skill. Whatever way she aims however, she is sure to reach the end result, with very few exceptions. Take your time with your partner. If you ask her questions and learn the moves that rock her world, you are guaranteed a player's pass to return to the field every time. Rush her consistently and you will be blocked from entering the stadium.

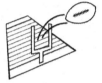

Fun Football Fact:
Which player was the first recorded in NFL history to reach a career high of the most safeties?

· Women want to be respected, so don't use the words "chick" or "broad" or any other unflattering nouns as part of your regular vocabulary. That's a personal foul!

· Don't leave the health of the relationship entirely up to your partner. She will eventually give up because it hurts her to consistently try to communicate her needs and desires or try to figure out yours without your help. She will feel like she is the only one who cares about them. She needs to know that you are actively participating or she will become frustrated.

· Say "I love you" without any hidden agenda. Love doesn't mean "sex" so don't use it to get some. We've heard that line before!

· Silence is deadly. If a woman is silent for too long, there is a problem. Get in the game before you are kicked out.

· Avoid the use of phrases such as: "It's a waste of time!" "You never..." "You always..." or "Why don't you ever..." and so on when in a heated argument. These negative statements will crush her spirit. There is no "waste of time" when it comes to a relationship and "absolute" statements are often merely exaggerations and completely unproductive. Women, this holds true for you as well; in fact, women are generally more guilty of using these phrases than men. Remember that you can never take back such words and you can't usually get back what you've emotionally thrown away.

Fun Football Fact:
Bill McPeak of the Pittsburgh Steelers reached a career high of the most safeties. What years did he play?
From 1949-1957.

· Don't make jokes about something that she feels is important. Just because it's not important to you does not mean it's not important for her. You are devaluing her and perhaps destroying any future emotional or physical contact if you do this consistently. If you discredit what she says by claiming that it is not important, the relationship will eventually disintegrate.

· Appreciate her. Just as you like to be appreciated when you clean the toilet, you need to show the same regard for her. It's important to always say "thank you." Don't stop praising her once you are married. Remember, it's not her responsibility to feed you and clean the house. There is nothing in any playbook and there is nothing biblically that says it's only her job. Instead, she does it because she loves you. If you love her back, she will appreciate you. If she weren't there to do it for you, you would be doing it alone. No team of any kind is fully functional with only one player.

· A small compliment goes a long way. It will make her feel appreciated. If you make it a daily ritual to compliment her and tell her how beautiful you think she is, you will be winning points with her daily.

Fun Football Fact:
Which two teams set the record for most turnovers in one game in NFL history?

· Clean the house with her. Make it a game. Each partner picks a room of equal size and works on it. The person who gets their room cleaned first, doing a good job, tells the other partner what piece of clothing they must remove-- each partner must wear the same amount of clothing. The person who loses their clothing first, and once the entire house is clean, must then do the bidding of their partner. With so much clothing already off, it's a perfect time to shower together. If you have children, of course you will have to modify this.

· Don't ever tell unflattering jokes about your partner. You may think they're funny, but they won't be to her. She will view these jokes as criticism and you will deeply hurt and offend her. Eventually, she will start to pull away from you. Look for her non-verbal cues.

· If you treat other people or things better than you treat her, she will feel you are devaluing her.

· Don't treat her roughly with something she is concerned about. Don't tell her to "get over it" or suggest that she needs to "toughen up." She is NOT a football player! If she is dealing with a matter that is important to her. You need to hear her concerns, even if you don't understand them, and just be there for her. If you treat her roughly in this area, she will start to distrust you with her feelings and your relationship will suffer greatly. You will close her down and she will be very unresponsive to you in every way, especially sexually.

Fun Football Fact:
The Chicago Bears versus the Detroit Lions game had the most turnovers at 17 on November 22, 1942. However, four years later, this record was tied on December 8, 1946 when the Boston Yanks played the Philadelphia Eagles.

· Be tender with her in non-sexual ways. This will help to soften her spirit if there is any problem. Remember that Jesus used touch to heal the sick and cure the lame, as did Mother Theresa and Princess Diana. And, although they didn't cure anyone, necessarily, they did touch lives and inspire miracles. So too can your touch help to heal a wounded spirit when done in a loving manner.

· Always apologize, even if you aren't the one who has committed the foul. Don't wait for the coin toss to determine which team goes first. Be proactive when dealing with any argument or conflicted situation. Saying something to the effect of, "I'm sorry that we are quarreling; can we work out a solution?" is not admitting to a tactical error on your part but will open the lines of communication so that you can both resolve the issue. If you find that you weren't sensitive to her needs, say something like, "I'm sorry I wasn't hearing what you were saying or being sensitive to your needs." (The meaning of "sensitive" is, "Susceptible to the attitude, feelings, or circumstances of others. xxii") Whoever gets the ball into play by apologizing first, will usually have the advantage. You will gain additional yards towards your goal of a touchdown if you swallow your pride and make the first move in the healing process. *"...with all lowliness and meekness, with patience, forbearing one another in love, eager to maintain the unity of the Spirit in the bond of peace." Ephesians 4:2-3*

Fun Football Fact:
When did the first NFL divisional playoff game take place?

· Don't give lectures. Just as you don't want to be treated as a child, neither does she. *"Be completely humble and gentle: be patient, bearing with one another in love." Ephesians 4:2*

· Try to avoid offering solutions unless your partner specifically asks you to help her. Generally speaking, men want solutions, while woman want sympathy. When your partner comes to you with something that has happened during her day, she might not always want a solution, but may just need some understanding and an active listener.

· Not all women gossip and many don't trust men who do.

· Value her. The meaning of "value" is, "to regard highly; to esteem. [xxiii] "

More on Women

· Women are sensitive and vulnerable. It's what makes us who we are and it's what drew you to us in the first place.

· Deeply kiss her every day. She will become highly responsive to your needs if you make kissing a priority in your relationship.

· When kissing her, however, don't use the toilet brush method mentioned above. Thrusting your tongue into her mouth and swishing it around constantly is highly annoying, to say the least. Use your lips as if they were your hands. Gently massage her lips with yours. Ask her how she likes to be kissed and have her show you. Practice makes perfect!

On the flip side, here are a few things men would like women to know about them and the way they think. These are all sentiments expressed on numerous surveys. In some cases, I am going to include the actual response from one or more of the surveys because I thought the responses were interesting and well put; I believe that changing it wouldn't have as much impact.

I am a woman after all and think like a woman. Changing the way a statement has been made by a man in some cases, would then create them into my interpretation of the words as a woman. I believe it is important to see the words the men actually used and

Fun Football Fact:
The first NFL divisional playoff game took place on December 14, 1941. The Chicago Bears beat the Green Bay Packers 33 - 14!.

the manner in which they used them. Pay close attention to the way the words were used by the men to better understand their thought process. I hope that the following survey answers add a little insight. Note that most men gave a lot more than five answers for each question with many answers achieving a strong consensus. Therefore, I've included a number of the most popular answers.

1.   What are the top five things that women do that make you crazy or get on your nerves?

· Manipulate.

· "Two words... MOOD SWINGS!"

· "Say... 'Whatever YOU want to do...' when truth is, that translates into 'you had better do what I WANT to do and you BETTER know what that is!'"

· Complain too much.

· "Women who are always trying to solve my problems make me crazy! Here's the deal. Sometimes, men sort out their problems by speaking about them out loud. When a woman hears the problem, they have to tell you what to do and then nag you until you do it. That's why a man never shares his feelings."

· Women who are distracted.

· Women who aren't straightforward or refuse to speak plainly.

· Women who are constantly trying to change things.

· Women who are needy and constantly arguing for "my" attention.

2.   What top five things would you want a woman to know more about concerning men?

· If you don't mean it, then don't say it! (This resounded through out both the male and female surveys and was the number one answer on both!)

Fun Football Fact:
What year was the first recorded college football - soccer game ever?

· That "men are really simple," yet they do have "complex souls."

· If you come to talk, be prepared to listen.

· Compromise is a "two-way street."

· "Say what you really mean, not what you think we want to hear. We are grown men... we can take it."

· Men listen differently than women.

· That men know, but don't always admit, when they aren't right. Why? Because..."Sometimes a decision must be made."

The following response was an answer to the above question, but I wanted to include it here in its entirety to help women see a man's thoughts clearly. This same idea was put in a number of ways by different men, but wasn't necessarily at the top of the list of things that men want us to know about them.

> *Response:* "That we are observant. We do notice your new hair cut; we just don't want to talk about it."

3. What do you wish women would do more consistently when they are dealing with you?

· "Say what they reeeeeally mean!!!!" (This was the over whelming number one answer and actually the one nearly 93% of the men put with no other answer.)

The following is an example taken from one of the surveys that gives a great illustration of what men are talking about above. See if this scenario sounds familiar.

"If you want something, tell us what it is; don't make us guess. Here's a story. My girlfriend and I were watching a chick movie and she said to me, 'I think I want some ice cream.' A little while later, she said, 'Do we have any ice cream in the freezer?' A while after that, she said, 'Ice cream and a movie, they sure go good together.'

By then, she sounded as if she was getting angry, but calmed down then said, 'Do you want ice cream?' I didn't, so I said, 'No thanks.' By then, it was the final straw for her and she snapped at me. 'Why don't you listen to me when I ask you for ice cream!!' I was bewildered because she never asked me for a bowl of ice cream. All she had to say was, 'Can you get up and get me bowl of ice cream, please?' I would have then known that she actually wanted me to get up and get the bowl of ice cream for her and would have done it!"

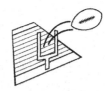

Fun Football Fact:
What year were the first American Football rules written?

4. ***When a woman says, "Can we talk please?" what is the first thing that goes through your mind?***

· "That she is about to complain about something."

· "What did I do wrong?" (These first two responses again were overwhelming winners.)

· "Is there going to be room for compromise or is this a lose-lose situation where a gallon of ice cream might help me smooth this over?
(Does Baskin-Robbins deliver... help!)"

5. ***A woman in your life talks to you about a problem that is hers. How do you respond and why?***

There were actually only three answers to this question given by all the men, but put in a variety of ways. Again, I am going to use their actual responses.

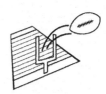

Fun Football Fact:
The first American Football rules were written in 1876. It was also during that year the "Father of American Football," Walter Camp, first became involved with the game.

· "I listen. I analyze and absorb the information. I try in my own way to 'solve' the problem. I share my advice on the situation. I stop if it seems that I am being insensitive. I try to 'fix' my problems and therefore want to 'fix' those that belong to my loved ones."

· "I always try to solve the problem and give them a solution. I think men are excellent problem solvers, but that's the way we were brought up.

· "I need to listen to the problem and let them figure it out."

· "Let her talk it out and use me as a mirror. Not to fix her problem but, let her try out her own solutions on me."

6.   *Why do you think that men have better friendships with another man than with a woman?*

For this question, it was harder to analyze the data and give a direct answer, so I am just going to put down a few of the responses taken directly from the surveys.

· "The same reason that women have trouble being friends with other women. Why is it that women say they get along better with men than other women?"

· "Men talk about sex or cars. They know and understand these when "relating" to each other on an interpersonal level. Women talk about emotions and things that require mental stimulation. I get enough of that at work. Men just want to talk and usually keep the talk to one or two subject matters at the very most. When women talk, they expect you to lis ten and usually talk about a multitude of subjects all at once. I am tired at the end of the day and I don't want to be required to listen to one more problem or try to listen to more than one or two subjects at a time."

7.   *Why do you think men and women are different?*

Again, the responses basically boiled down to two different reasons. One is our physiological make-up and the other involves our history and the way we were each individually raised. I am posting a few of the answers that I feel best sum up what the other surveys said so, as previously stated, that you can see the exact words men that men use.

· "Partially hormones, but I do believe it is also based on the way we are raised that makes us different."

· "Women and men are confused about their roles and responsibilities in life. We are created differently."

· "No getting around it... our biology will always influence our thinking processes."

Here are a few more things that men want women to know:

· "We love to be there for you; let us be men and do that.
  You don't have to have all of the answers."

· "Don't always bring up what you think we can do to better
  ourselves. We know that, but we may like the way we are."

· "Accept us exactly the way we are; we aren't going to change
  once you "get us" in a relationship. We are who we are."

· "Love does not always mean the same thing to us that it does
  to you. Remember that." (This one came up a lot in the
  surveys, so be warned women. It comes directly from their
  mouths!) "Sometimes, we just want quick, fast sex. That's it.
  It helps us relieve tension."

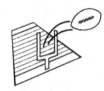

Fun Football Fact:
What rule was passed regarding the "forward pass" in 1951?

· "If you want us to be romantic, help us know what romance
  means to you so we can achieve 'romance' the way you
  like it."

· "We can't read minds; don't expect us to know what
  you want."

· "Remind us when a special date is. If it's important to you,
  it's important to us as well."

So there you have a little insight into the worlds of both men
and women.

CHAPTER 13
The Chemistry of Love—Scientific Facts

Just as scientific data is gathered and analyzed to find out how athletes use their skeletal structures and muscles to improve their game, so too have scientists gathered information to better understand the science behind the word "love." So, what exactly are the "chemicals of love" or the "chemistry of love?"

As I said before, the beginning of a man's interest in a woman occurs when he perceives her to be visually beautiful and stimulating. The feelings that may occur once the two actually meet, however, really does deal with chemicals after all. When a man's brain registers desire, his hypothalamus gland, which is located deep within the center of the brain, begins to gather information. [xxiv] This gland then sends out signals through the man's central nervous system, which in turn cause the pituitary gland to make hormones setting off a sexual awakening.

This is a very powerful instigating force for a man and will generally cause him to make first contact with the woman that he desires. At that point, the man's entire cellular system begins to work together with the hypothalamus gland to initiate the responses needed for interaction. His body begins to heat up and his adrenaline begins to pump, causing his skin to flush, his heart to beat faster, his hands to become sweaty and his breathing to become heavier. He also begins to take in more oxygen during this process.

If he is successful in interacting with the woman of his desire in a positive fashion, his brain responds by releasing endorphins, which are chemicals that help inhibit pain and produce a feeling of happiness. When the endorphins are released from the center of the brain, they act as a catalyst, triggering other cells to naturally excrete Phenylethylamine, another type of endorphin. [xxv]

Fun Football Fact:
On January 18, 1951 a rule was passed that stated that no tackle, guard or center would be eligible to catch a forward pass.

Phenylethylamine then helps initiate the release of dopamine and oxytocin, which triggers the euphoric feeling that many men and women experience after sex. While research has shown that dopamine is mainly released in men during sexual activity, it is also released in small dosages within a woman's system. [xxvi] This invigorating chemical cocktail is capable of dominating any brain activity that governs rational thinking, something that many people can attest to. Phenylethylamine is known as "the love drug" and Oxytocin is sometimes referred to as "the cuddle drug."

Phenylethylamine produces the "high" that we obtain when we are in love. It's the substance that causes us to be excessively happy during that period. By contrast, it is believed that people who don't have enough Phenylethylamine in their chemical make-up tend to be more depressed than those with a normal dose. We are charged with an abundance of energy whenever Phenylethylamine is produced. In fact, even chocolate produces small amounts of this endorphin. It's my theory that somewhere back in time, when chocolate was first discovered, someone noticed the happy feeling that resulted from eating it and a new phenomenon was born.

Wanting to have a better outcome with their intended, men began to bring along chocolate to help entice their loved one, using it as a mild aphrodisiac and starting the tradition of chocolates as a gift when going out on a date. Because chocolate contains low levels of Phenylethylamine, it may also be the reason why so many people reach for a chocolate bar when their love is unrequited.

Research has shown that Oxytocin is also secreted by the pituitary gland and produces a feeling of satisfaction, inducing a calming effect. It also produces nurturing instincts. It is believed that Oxytocin helps with deepening and maintaining interpersonal relationships, directly affecting how well we bond with one another. Oxytocin is released in women after sex and studies show that it may remain in the bloodstream for up to two weeks after a sexual encounter. This is yet another reason to win points with the woman in your life! Remember, "Happy wife! Happy Life!"

Last but not least, our mixture of love contains pheromones, which are used to silently transmit messages to the opposite sex amongst most species of animals, including humans. Scientists are still trying to discover more about how human pheromones actually work. They do know that the entire chemical chain reaction happens instantaneously for a man, while in a woman, the process is more like the aging of a fine wine. For women, the chemical process is similar to that for a man, but the sexual attraction begins in her brain and does not necessarily produce an instantaneous reaction. When Phenylethylamine and Oxytocin come together to form a sort of chemical cocktail of love and attraction, it can be an overwhelming experience. Because this chemical cocktail has been shown to create a feeling of closeness and "love," it is my theory that this may be the reason why so many men rely on sex to create bonding in their life. Again, due to their lack of the same type of nurturing that women receive during their formative years and because this chemical cocktail creates a sense of bonding, it may be the only way that men initially know how to reach out. However, as I pointed out earlier, this does not mean that men must continue with this approach.

While these chemicals bring truth to the saying "love at first sight," I would prefer to call it "attraction at first sight." That's what it really is. The "chemistry of love" has actually been handed down through our evolutionary chain.

Fun Football Fact:
Which team has won the most games in NFL history?

Researchers have found that throughout the world, men and women are attracted subconsciously to people who will help to improve their DNA when proliferating our species. When men and women are looking for a mate, their subconscious has a lot of control over their decision-making process. For example, studies have shown that men are subconsciously attracted to women with broader hips, which scientists theorize to mean that broader hips signal fertility to the male brain.

Women, meanwhile, are subconsciously attracted to broader shoulders as this signals strength. Additionally, both sexes subconsciously look for symmetry in facial features. Michael Mills, a psychology professor at Loyola Marymount University in Los Angeles, has this to say about facial symmetry: "When we see asymmetrical features, it's a suggestion of a genetic defect or a developmental problem, so we tend to avoid those people as love objects. [xxvii]"

Basically, Michael Mills theorizes that our subconscious minds perceive asymmetrical features as being genetically flawed and may cause us to shy away from another person in order to inhibit reproduction of what our subconscious mind perceives as a faulty gene. It's survival of the fittest, so to speak, mimicking the animal kingdom.

Jumping for Joy

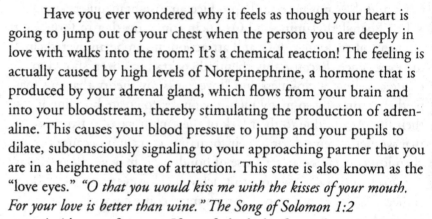

Fun Football Fact:
The Chicago Bears have 632 wins, the most in NFL History.

Have you ever wondered why it feels as though your heart is going to jump out of your chest when the person you are deeply in love with walks into the room? It's a chemical reaction! The feeling is actually caused by high levels of Norepinephrine, a hormone that is produced by your adrenal gland, which flows from your brain and into your bloodstream, thereby stimulating the production of adrenaline. This causes your blood pressure to jump and your pupils to dilate, subconsciously signaling to your approaching partner that you are in a heightened state of attraction. This state is also known as the "love eyes." *"O that you would kiss me with the kisses of your mouth. For your love is better than wine." The Song of Solomon 1:2*

A side note for men: If you feel a lack of sexual motivation, you might want to check with your doctor to see if you should be taking zinc supplements. Studies have shown that zinc is the single most important nutrient for a man's sexuality and will increase your testosterone levels. These are the facts of the "chemistry of love."

CHAPTER 14
Illegal Procedures—Women in the Wallet, Women in the Frames

The quickest way to build solid walls between you and your partner is to do what I call the "Women in the Wallet, Women in the Frames." Put quite simply, this is the displaying of other women in a place of honor, such as with a prominently displayed photograph. In a game of football, an "illegal procedure" is used to indicate any number of infractions that may occur before the snap of the ball. When you place an old girlfriend or crush in a place of honor, such as your wallet or in a picture frame on your desk or wall, you are making an "illegal procedure" in your relationship.

One of the biggest mistakes that men make in their relationships is to dishonor their partner by openly displaying their lust for another woman. While there will be many men who disagree with this entire chapter, if you want to stay on the team roster and avoid being cut for another player, pay close attention to the details I write about in this chapter and consider yourself warned.

One of the leading causes of splits in a relationship is infidelity. Why do affairs begin? It all comes down to a demise of communication. The collapse of a relationship begins with the breakdown of communication followed by one party dishonoring their partner, eventually leading to a buildup of distrust and resentment and eventually a lack of interest in the bedroom.

While many would say their infidelity was a direct result of their partner's behavior towards them, declaring that their partner caused the loss of "love" in the relationship, this statement is not altogether true. The unfaithful partner was the one who committed the serious betrayal of trust and is ultimately responsible for the ensuing problems that follow, including divorce.

Fun Football Fact:
What relevance does the date January 24, 1953 have in regards to football?

In addition to breaking the bond of trust, he has risked the life of his partner with the possible introduction of a deadly, sexually transmitted disease. While I am not implying that men are the only ones who are unfaithful, since this book is geared mostly for men, I think that using "he" in this example is more appropriate.

While men are visually stimulated and chemicals do have a large effect on their reactions to women, that does not give a man permission to stare at every woman who walks by or shows up on their television screen. Why even put yourself in a situation where there is temptation? There is no "just because I'm on a diet doesn't mean I can't look at the menu" excuse acceptable for this situation. If you want to look at the menu, you had better get take-out, because it won't be long before you are kicked out of the bedroom and then off the team entirely.

Recently, I was sitting with a couple who seemingly had a warm and loving relationship. An ad came across the television screen displaying several scantily clad women. The man said, "Oh my!" and raised his eyebrows. He immediately noticed his behavior and quickly turned to begin complimenting his partner.

Even so, I could see the hurt in the woman's eyes when she turned away. While she is considered to be a "hottie" by most men and logically, this slight lapse in judgment shouldn't bother her, I could see trouble was on the horizon. Even to a casual outside observer such as me, I heard the lust in his voice and saw the gleam in his eyes; even more, her reaction led me to believe this may not have been an isolated case, but a consistent behavior.

There is a difference between "noticing" and "looking." Women understand "noticing," even if it does twinge at their heart some, but gawking is another matter entirely. It is very dishonoring to a woman when the man she is with gawks at another woman. Even the most incredibly beautiful woman with a flawless body and perfect features can have her spirit crushed by this kind of behavior. Another couple that I was interviewing had a very cold and businesslike relationship. I noticed as I spent time with them that the husband had pictures of naked women pasted all over his house as well as on the dashboard of his truck. When I inquired as to why he had these posted all over the place, he said that his wife had given him these pictures as a Christmas present. Many of the pictures scattered throughout his daily life were taken from *Playboy* and *Penthouse* as well as various nude calendars and photograph journals.

Fun Football Fact: January 24, 1953 signifies the date when the names of the American and National conferences were changed to the Eastern and Western conferences.

After spending a little bit of time with them, I began to notice the lack of any physical touch or contact between the two. On our second meeting, I asked the wife why she subscribed to these magazines for her husband. Her response shocked me as I had assumed that she did so because she didn't mind him looking at other naked women. Her response, however, had nothing to do with that at all. Instead, she told me that it kept him away from her. He laughed it off, but I could see a little bit of puzzlement behind his eyes.

I then concentrated on the husband and asked him why he thought she made such a statement. He explained that they didn't have much of a sex life because she didn't like sex. So, to make him happy, she had given him these magazines and other pornographic material. I won't go into details other than to say that he and his magazines and photographs had developed an entire life of their own together. You get the picture - no pun intended. Eventually, the real story came out. She said that he consistently criticized her for being overweight and complained that she didn't look like the women he would see displayed in ad's, on television and in various periodicals. (By the way, he was equally heavy, with his own Buddha Belly.)

Fun Football Fact: When was the Super Bowl Trophy renamed for the famous coach, Vince Lombardi?

Because of his constant criticism and comparisons to the women that he idolized, she completely lost interest in him and any sexual contact with him in any way was repulsive to her. She also stated that he really wasn't interested in how she felt in bed and would tell her he knew what to do and didn't need her advice.

In order to make him happy, she decided to help him fulfill his fantasy of the perfect woman by subscribing to the magazines noted above and giving him the calendars and photographs of nude women. By doing this, it also kept her from having to have contact with her husband. When I asked him how he felt about her response, he said she obviously didn't really mind or she wouldn't be allowing him to participate in his "fantasies."

He apparently did not "hear" or understand the gravity of the situation and wanted to continue to live in lala land. This was a relationship in deep trouble on so many levels. The affects of his "relationship" with these fantasy women were strewn all over his real life relationship with his wife. What this man had not admitted to himself yet, was the fact that if he didn't curb his enthusiasm for his "fantasy" woman, he would continue to have only a "fantasy" relationship with a flat piece of paper and celluloid as cold as his marriage. He had completely lost sight of what a really fulfilling and happy relationship is or perhaps he had never known what that means. He hadn't yet made the decision to make his relationship go

Fun Football Fact:
On September 10, 1970 the Super Bowl trophy was renamed the Vince Lombardi Trophy.

Fun Football Fact:
Which kicker has the best percentage of field goals in NFL history?

from cold to red hot. This couple needed to take a deep look into their relationship and learn why it had denigrated so far; the husband also needed to stop his worship of women who are not real. Most of these women presented in the magazines are airbrushed; if you approached them in real life, you'd notice the cellulite and wrinkles as well as the fat pockets just like any other human being.

While many men would LOVE to have a woman who was more than happy for him to indulge in pornography with her blessing, just like this woman was doing, what they don't realize is that this leads to the deterioration of their real relationship. Eventually, such men will be left with either their fantasy or a woman who may have emotional problems, such as the woman above. Some of those problems may stem from her childhood. Issues that may have never been fully addressed or resolved. Additionally, she may be totally lacking in self esteem or self respect from other incidents that have occurred in her life.

While the media often glamorizes strip clubs, adult film stars and prostitution, if you were to really look into the lives and relationships of these people, you would see that their lives aren't very fulfilling and their relationships don't tend to last.

Every one that I have ever interviewed or seen interviewed have all had sad stories to tell. While seemingly independent, well-adjusted and externally happy, looking deeper into their personalities and lives reveals that they are really unhappy and have had some event in their past life that has led them down the dark roads of depression and into the world of pornography, drugs, alcohol. Many eventually commit suicide, believing it is their only way out of the world they are in. Whether as an audience member (most women stated that they view pornography and/or go to strip clubs to gain acceptance from whomever they are with or to appear "hip." Remember the survey.) or as a participant (again used to gain acceptance and find what they perceive to be "love,") each one of these women that I have interviewed or seen interviewed, whether they are in the industry or just casual observers, have insecurity issues that they haven't been able to reconcile yet. While money may be an initial motivating factor for some participants, they also need the accolades to affirm who they are and they secretly feel that this is all they deserve.

I recently watched a special on television with one of the most popular adult film stars today. Her life appears to be full of glamour and fun on the outside, but upon further inspection, is actually filled with turmoil and self-hatred.

She has made a truckload of money and has a handsome and adoring husband and family (parent and sibling) as well as a lot of admiring and faithful fans. She is drop dead gorgeous, with a killer body and a seemingly sweet spirit, yet she has struggled with self-esteem her entire life. These issues are what led her into pornography and the eventual use and overdose of drugs and alcohol.

When asked during the interview about whether she and her husband would have children themselves, she said that she wanted a family desperately, and she would stop any activity in the adult industry once she had kids. The interviewer then asked her if her children decided they wanted to pursue a career in the adult entertainment industry, would she be agreeable with their decision. She gave a very emphatic "no." She said she did not want them to participate in it once they were old enough to make those types of decisions.

My questions was, why would someone who seems to be absolutely fine with her choice to participate in pornography and actually celebrates it in the interview; someone who has received a tremendous amount of money as well as a lot of accolades from around the world for her work in the industry; not want her children to participate in a career that has given her so much?

The answer is that she knows firsthand that it leads to a lot of personal tribulations not shown on television, with depression and deep self-loathing being just a few of those problems.

I want to say that I do not think that prostitutes, people in the adult entertainment business or strippers are any better or worse than the rest of us, nor do I believe they are "bad" people. They have simply made choices in their lives that are deeply hurting them emotionally, physically (look at the outbreak of AIDS in the news recently in adult film industry even with all of the "protection" they administer before shooting the film), and spiritually whether or not they have decided to deal with the issues or not. But, let me get to a tamer example of self-esteem and how someone dishonoring you can affect it. Let's say that you are a kicker for the New York Jets and you are considered an extremely valuable player who always comes through for his team. You work harder than most of the other members of your team and never miss a practice or a game.

However, despite all of your hard work, your coach is consistently making flattering comments about other kickers on opposing teams, praising them for their hard work and occasionally implying that it would be great to get them onto his team. Rarely does he look over to you and say "good work." Over time, you might begin to feel insecure about your position on the team, wondering if you might be cut and whether someone else might be drafted into your position. Let me give another, more pragmatic example. You work in the corporate world and have had your eye on a position in your company for a long time. Eventually you are promoted to your dream job. After all of your hard work in your new position, however, you begin to notice that your boss is no longer appreciating the extra hours you have been putting in. He no longer praises you for a "job well done" quite as often as he did before. You do notice, however, that he looks over at your colleagues and offers praise and pats on the back to them. If this continues, eventually, you are bound to feel like your position is in jeopardy. I guarantee it.

When men stare and make comments about other women, they cause the exact same reaction in their partner. Let me reverse the tables. You and your wife have been married for a few years. Your wife makes a habit of watching bodybuilding contests or subscribes to *Playgirl* under the pretense that it has great articles that are very educational.

Mind you, there are very educational and beneficial articles in *The Wall Street Journal* and *The New York Times*, but those aren't the publications that are on her coffee table. You are a fairly well-built man yourself, but you watch her spend time that she could be investing with you by looking through the pages of *Playgirl*, ogling at the men inside with a huge smile on her face and giving an occasional grunt or comment about their firm abs and tight derrières. I guarantee you that, after a few months of this type of behavior, possibly even just a few weeks, you would become jealous and insecure about your position in her life. While noticing another woman non-overtly is a natural reaction, there is no excuse for a man who is in a relationship to lust after other women or vice versa.

Turning your head to stare and/or make comments about another woman or man is the fastest way to dishonor your partner and breed distrust. It will eventually lead to the demise of your relationship and you will most certainly be cut from the team roster if you continue with this kind of behavior.

An acquaintance of mine has several pictures of old girlfriends in his wallet. He has been married for five years and his marriage is in shambles. It hurts his wife deeply that he keeps the pictures in his wallet. When I challenged him on this, his excuse was "Why should it bother her? I didn't marry any of them. Besides, they were all in there before I met her." My response to him: "Why do you need them in your wallet? Obviously, there is a reason why you didn't

Fun Football Fact:
The kickers with the best percentage of field goals in the NFL are Olindo Mare and Mike Vanderjagt. Olindo Mare also holds the record for the most fieldgoals in one season at 39! At a close second, Jeff Wilkins with 37 field goals in one season.

marry them. Is it okay if I go through your wife's old photo albums and pull out pictures of old boyfriends she had and put them in her wallet?" With this last question, he turned and walked away. Because he did not see any reason why he should change his old habits or take the old flames away from the fire to extinguish them, they ultimately ended up in divorce court. Men who continue these behaviors will find themselves alone or with a woman who has little or no self-esteem or respect for herself.

I know another man who keeps a picture of himself cuddling a professional model in a frame on his mantle. While I know this woman is only an acquaintance of his and not interested in him romantically, he keeps it on the shelf as if she were his girlfriend. Why does he do that? By his own admission, he thinks that if other women believe he can "get" a woman like that, it will make him more desirable in their eyes. What he doesn't realize is that he is raising the level of insecurity of any potential girlfriend. Such insecurity invariably leads to resentment and then hostility, which always affects the way she views and treats him.

It is never okay to have old flames hanging in picture frames or stuffed in your wallet, both of which are places of honor. Additionally, it is not okay for men to attend strip clubs or subscribe to "girly" magazines, unless they want to watch their relationship wither and die. Remember the survey in an earlier chapter? The choice is yours: keep those pictures in a place of honor and watch your partner eventually say goodbye or keep your partner, put out your old flames and place them in storage.

A side note to women: Forget playing games! Trying to make the man in your life jealous in order to elicit more attention from him will eventually backfire. You too must remember what the survey said. Men don't like women who manipulate. If you need more attention, gently ask for it. If that doesn't grab his attention, create an emotional word picture to help you communicate your needs.

Fun Football Fact:
Which two teams have both led the NFL in penalties for the most consecutive seasons?

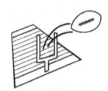

Fun Football Fact:
The Chicago Bears and the Oakland Raiders tie with the most penalties in consecutive seasons. The Chicago Bears led the league for four seasons twice, first from 1941-44 and then again between 1946-49. The Oakland Raiders had four seasons also. Their consecutive seasons were from 1993-96.

CHAPTER 15
Adding Value to Your Team—
Spending and Investing Time

When teams draft a player, they do so to add value to the group. They invest large sums of money and clusters of time on the potential of their new draftee. They don't do this in the hope that the new player will warm the benches or be used to fill an already overcrowded locker room. Instead, they do it to hopefully raise the bar and better the team's chances for a shot at the Super Bowl.

When you become part of a relationship, you do so to add value to your quality of life and be part of a team. You don't enter into a relationship to go it alone or be left out of the game. Just as teams invest time and money on their draft picks, it is also very important that couples spend and invest time together on a regular basis in order to build a strong relationship. The activities that you do together can be anything that either one of you enjoys doing.

In this chapter, I will be using two different phrases: "spending time" and "investing time." Spending time implies the action of giving time away. If you are spending time by doing something that is mutually satisfying to you both, you have chosen to give your time away to someone special in your life, thereby making them feel important.

Fun Football Fact:
Who was the announcer for a first national radio broadcast NFL game?

A shared hobby or a sport can do wonders to create warmth and closeness in an otherwise lagging relationship. However, because your interests may differ somewhat, make sure that you both get equal time in the decision-making process.

Investing time implies the action of committing to something in order to gain more value. This not only makes someone feel they are important in your life, but it makes them feel treasured and adds special value to their life because you are investing time on a more

Fun Football Fact:
On November 29th, 1934, Graham McNamee was the announcer for the NFL's first broadcast game. The game was broadcast on NBC radio and featured the Chicago Bears against the Detroit Lions.

intimate and personal level. It usually involves finding out what they think about certain things, such as life, politics or love. Investing time sometimes involves sitting silently; gazing into each other's eyes while holding hands. It can also be cuddling on the couch, sharing personal thoughts and ideas.

Spending time usually consists of going to the movies or out to a restaurant. Why do I put these activities under the category of "spending time?" Let's face it; unless you like food flying out of someone's mouth or you don't care if your partner eats cold food so that they can talk to you, a restaurant is not a good place to attempt any deep communication. In contrast, going out for a cappuccino would fall under my category of investing time. What is the difference? You don't have to rush to eat in between words so your food won't get cold and there are no worries of food flying out of your mouth or a waiter or waitress constantly interrupting your train of thought. Having an in depth conversation is more feasible while holding a hot cup of coffee in your hand.

A side note: Once a man is deeply entrenched in a relationship, he may think that spending and investing time is all about working on the roof, painting the house or fixing the car, however, women do not think of it in the same way. While a woman deeply appreciates all of those actions and everything that you do for her, those actions are in the same category for her as taking your dry cleaning in, making your lunch, running the finances, doing your laundry, cleaning the house or raising the children. They are jobs and responsibilities that you both, as a team, must do to maintain equilibrium in your lives. They have nothing to do with spending quality time together or building up your relationship.

Since I often hear, even amongst my girlfriends, expressions like, "Well, what should we do tonight?" I thought that I would list a few things here to make the selection process easier. Hopefully, you won't get caught up doing the same thing for every date night.

Spending Time—A List of Things to Do

Fun Football Fact:
When was the first overtime NFL game?

Fun, Free or Inexpensive Ways to Spend Time (This list is all about having fun, but is not conducive to extensive verbal communication.)

Go ice-skating on a pond	Take a motorcycle ride
Go for a swim	Go jogging
Listen to music	Meet your neighbors

Read a book out loud to each other
Go to a theater in the park
Play Frisbee
Play soccer
Go rafting
Ride bikes
Go roller-skating
Go snorkeling
Go tubing
Go water-skiing
Workout at home or the gym
Go to the drive-in movies and have a barbecue while watching the movie
Go to Macy's or some other department store to listen to the pianist.

Listen to music in the park
Play touch football
Play games (board games, cards, etc.)
Rent a movie
Go roller-blading
Go jet skiing
Go surfing
Watch a movie on television or pop one you already own in your VCR or DVD player.
Go to the water slides at a national park (they are less expensive than one specifically for water slides)

Fun Football Fact:
The first overtime NFL game occurred on August 28, 1955. In a preseason game, the Los Angeles Rams beat the New York Giants 23 - 17 three minutes into overtime.

Fun Ways to Spend Time with Money

Go horseback riding
Go bowling
Go cross-country skiing
Go kayaking
Go roller-skating at a rink
Go to a football game
Go to the movies
Go to an ice-skating show
Join an outdoor club together
Play laser tag
Run a race together
Go snowmobiling
Go to the symphony
Go on a dinner cruise
Take a massage class together
Take a martial arts class together
Go to a theme park

Go to the ballet
Go to a concert
Go ice-skating at a rink
Go out for pizza
Go to a baseball game
Go to a hockey game
Go to dinner
Go to a luxury spa
Join an activity club together
Go rock climbing
Go scuba diving
Go down hill snow skiing
Take a dancing class
Get a facial together
Get a couple's massage
Go to the theater
Go to a water slide park

Fun Football Fact:
When was the first Pro Bowl played?

Investing Time—A List of Things to Do

Fun, Free or Inexpensive Ways to Invest Time (this list is all about having fun as well, but is conducive to extensive verbal communication.)

Fun Football Fact:
The first Pro Bowl was played on January 15, 1939. The New York Giants played the Pro All-Stars and defeated them 13 - 10.

Barbecue (grill out)
Check out farms
Dance in your living room
Feed the ducks
Go out for a cappuccino
Go see fireworks
Go to a pet store
Go to an art gallery
Go to the park and swing
Go canoeing
Get involved in a fundraiser together
Have a snowball fight
Go hiking
Learn about the stars and
    constellations together
Make a tent in your living room
    and camp out
Put a photo album together and
    share the memories
Sit under the stars
Take a bath by candlelight
Take a scenic drive
Talk over hot cocoa
Walk by the beach or a lake
Walk the dog

Build a sand castle
Curl up next to a fire
Dare to dream together
Go fishing
Go out for ice cream
Go to a chess cafe
Go to a petting zoo
Go to historic sights
Build a snowman
Fly a kite
Have a chili cook-off
Have a water fight
Have a picnic
Learn an instrument together
Learn to cook something
Paint a picture together
Plant a garden
Plan and share ideas for your
    dream house
Study the Bible
Get in a Jacuzzi
Take a walk holding hands
Volunteer for community
    work

Fun Ways to Invest Time with Money

Play golf
Go dancing
Go to a festival
Go to a fair
Learn a sport together
Go paddle boating
Take a balloon ride
Take a train ride

Go camping
Spend the night at a
    bed & breakfast
Go to the zoo
Go miniature golfing
Go sailing
Take a class together
Take a weekend trip

There are many good ideas that you can expand upon or combine, as well. For example, build a tent in your living room, pop some popcorn, turn off the lights and pretend that you are camping. If you have a fireplace, build a fire and roast hot dogs and s'mores over it. Or rent a suite that has an indoor pool and spend the weekend in luxury together. Go to a spa that has a couple's massage area where they let you do massages on each other while you are in a fabulous rain room. It's an enchanting experience!

There are many more ways to spend and invest time together than the ones I have listed here. To make your ideas more cost effective, consider buying a two-for-one coupon book. Schools sell them every year in many towns across the U.S. Inside, you'll find buy-one-get-one-free offers and lists of everything from fast food places to fine dining establishments and resort spas. These books also have information and coupons for theme parks, Bed and Breakfast hotels, luxury spa resorts and other goods and services. They usually cost anywhere from $10 - $20, depending on the school, but will save you a lot of money, while also helping the schools in your community.

Recently I thought it would be fun to take my book along with $10 and see how far my money would go in feeding six people. Doing this experiment, my sister and I were able to purchase five barbecued bacon cheeseburgers, two chicken sandwiches, two large turkey subs, one large bag of French fries and one large soda from a variety of restaurants. Several people had multiple items and we still had leftovers to spare. It was a fun challenge that you and your partner can also do together.

Here are a few additional fun things that you can do to economize. Some banks have free cookies every Friday. For fun, you could go to all the different banks in your neighborhood and grab a cookie with your loved one. Or try going to Costco or Sam's Club and taste all the different samples they have. Most grocery stores also have daily free sample giveaways. Go to multiple See's candy stores and get free samples. Remember that chocolate can affect the " chemistry of love!" Go to all the car dealerships that are having free giveaways and have a test drive while stocking up on the free goodies! You can look on the Internet to find various other free giveaways too. Recently, Jamba Juice gave away free Smoothies and 7-11 gave away free slurpies for their anniversary date, July 11th (by the way, they do this every July 11th - 7-11).

There are a lot of fun things you can do for free if you do a little research. Libraries have most of the current videos available for

Fun Football Fact:
Who was the first man ever to be picked in the NFL draft and when was he chosen?

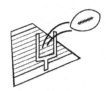

Fun Football Fact:
Halfback Jay Berwanger holds the distinction of being the first man to be picked in the NFL draft. The event took place on February 8, 1936. He also holds the merit of being the very first winner of the Heisman Trophy.

Fun Football Fact:
Who was the first person to openly accept compensation, technically becoming the first professional football player in history?

Fun Football Fact:
In 1895 John Brallier became the first football player to openly turn professional. Brallier accepted $10 to pay for expenses he incurred when playing with the Latrobe YMCA team. The opposing team? The Jeannette Athletic Club.

free checkout. Usually you don't have to return them for seven days and you can save on the cost of a rental. You can also check out current CDs and, of course, so many interesting books. While there, go to the information desk at the library and ask if they have any free tickets or discount coupons for local recreational and historical sights, museums and other attractions. Often local businesses, theme parks, museums and water parks give special passes to libraries. Many theme parks also have fifty cent or dollar days, so take advantage of these discounts.

Finally, here's a tip for anyone who really wants to get to know their partner relatively well-- take them camping. I am a firm believer that you should go camping with someone for at least 4 days before you get married. Why? Because when you are camping, everyone is out of their element. It's the best time to find out each others true character and personality.

There are no daily interruptions and, for the most part, no modern conveniences. You pitch a tent, cook your food over a fire, hang out with the gang and get to know each other. Since there are no televisions, telephones (unless someone cheats and brings their cell phone AND it has service where you are) or other distractions. You need to entertain each other naturally, by talking to one another. That's it. Showers are usually cold and the bathrooms far away. Facing these conditions, you will both get to know each other more intimately, helping determine if this is the person with whom you want to spend the rest of your life. While some marriages must be ended because of abuse and other extenuating circumstances, some are bad simply because the two people involved don't know each other and have built walls around themselves.

In those cases, marriage may be hard, but divorce is much harder, especially if there are children involved. So take the time to get to know each other before you make the jump.

CHAPTER 16
Looking For a Draw Play—
Nonverbal Communication

A draw play occurs when a pass is faked and the back carries the ball as the defensive linemen are drawn in for the pass rush. Someone who is good at keying might be able to anticipate this maneuver and block it. While the initial play was probably mapped out with verbal communication, it was executed with non-verbal commands. If the person keying catches onto the play, he must have picked up on the non-verbal cues. Just as the player caught onto the draw play from both the verbal and non-verbal cues, so too are there two different forms of communication in relationships: verbal and nonverbal.

Verbal communication is a learned response while nonverbal communication is all about body language and verbal tones. Whether it's arms crossed against our chests, smiles on our faces, a furrow in our brow or simply the tone of our voice, all of these actions communicate how we are feeling more than words do. The depth or intimacy of our interaction with each other depends on how much we know about each other's language.

All living creatures communicate and respond to nonverbal communication. For example, an elephant uses her trunk to nudge her baby underneath her. This communicates to the baby that there is danger and that the parent is watching out for her. A lioness crouches down low in the underbrush. This signals to the other lions in the pride that she's about to attack her prey. With humans, the use of nonverbal communication is no less important. A woman darts her eyes back and forth while someone is talking to her. This signals that she is not really interested in what the other person is saying or that she is distressed about something else. Nonverbal

Fun Football Fact:
Which NFL rookie became the first 1,000-yard rusher?

communication can speak volumes about what is going on at any given moment, ultimately accounting for a large part of meaningful communication. The way we sit, stand or make gestures to others helps them make a more accurate determination about what we are thinking and feeling as well as how we will respond to them. Gestures such as arms folded stiffly across our chest, legs crossed, narrowed eyes or tapping fingers all convey anger, frustration or distrust of the receiving party.

By contrast, smiling, intent eye contact, an open posture and gentle auditory tones all signal happiness and warmth directed towards the receiving party (much like a cat who kneads and purrs). Research shows that during our communication process, only seven percent of our communication occurs through verbal codes, while ninety-three percent is transmitted through nonverbal codes. Thirty-eight percent of this ninety-three percent is auditory, while another fifty-five percent is done with facial expressions and bodily gestures. xxviii

Many messages are sent subconsciously with nonverbal language. To help better understand nonverbal communication, we need to pay close attention to other people's body language or nonverbal cues and study them. While your partner may tell you that she is fine and that nothing is wrong, you must also listen to the sound of her voice and watch her body movements and facial expressions. These tones of voice and movements of the body tell you if everything really is fine or if there is something wrong that she is trying to mask. If you don't listen and watch for these cues, your relationship may eventually terminate. While words are easy to manipulate and can cover what is going on underneath, nonverbal communication is instinctual and therefore very hard to disguise. Here are a few examples of nonverbal communication and their respective meanings.

1. Looking directly into the eyes of the person you are addressing signals that you are confident.

2. Good posture also signals that you are confident.

3. A side hug signals that you are feeling discomfort or are not familiar with the recipient.

4. A frontal hug signals that you are at ease or familiar with the recipient.

Fun Football Fact:
In 1934, rookie Beattie Feathers of the Chicago Bears became the first rookie rusher in the NFL's to gain 1,000 yards. Feathers gained 1,004 on 101 carries.

Fun Football Fact:
When did the very first NFL championship game take place?

5. Avoiding eye contact signals insecurity or a lack of interest.

6. Looking down when another person is talking to you often signals distraction or rejection.

7. An open posture signals that you are receptive.

8. Arms folded tightly across your chest signals distrust, anger or frustration with the other person. (This applies unless, of course, you are in the arctic without a jacket. Then you are just cold!)

Here is an interesting trivia piece. Dr. Albert E. Scheflen discovered that when people agree with someone, they mimic the body language of that person. For example, if that person leans to the left, those in agreement also lean to the left. If that person crosses their legs, the others do the same.

Fun Football Fact:
The very first NFL championship game took place on December 17, 1933. The Chicago Bears played the New York Giants and defeated them 23 - 21.

CHAPTER 17
The Last Pass—How and Where to Meet the Woman or Man in Your Life If You Don't Currently Have Anyone to Score a Touchdown With

How do you meet the woman or man in your life if you haven't already done so? This is a hard question to answer. While this book is about relationships, it is not just for people who are already in a relationship, but also for those who are looking to have fulfilling relationships in the future.

If you don't already have a woman or a man in your life, it may seem extraordinarily hard to meet the right person. Maybe you've done the online dating scene and found that it isn't all that it's hyped up to be. Often, the people involved (men and women) don't measure up to their profiles or pictures.

Or perhaps they post information that is false or highly exaggerated, are looking for one-night stands even though they say they love long walks on the beach and are looking for a committed relationship or their picture was taken ten years ago when they were a teenager?

I have heard, as I'm sure that you have also, quite a few online dating nightmare stories. Perhaps because the general public looks at online dating as they would catalogue shopping, attempting to get the exact size, style, and look before they actually see the product. One man I spoke with struck up a conversation with a woman who wouldn't post her picture or send him one because she "didn't have one on her computer." She told him that he shouldn't worry because she was worth it.

Fun Football Fact:
Which NFL players have been multiple winners of the MVP award?

She also told him she was a lot younger than she was and very beautiful, setting up a set of expectations in his mind that if she had been honest about in the beginning, would not have been there. When the meeting night arrived, however, she was half an hour late. While he was anxiously waiting for her to arrive, he noticed every good-looking woman that walked in and his heart would race, hoping that it was her.

When she finally arrived, he was shocked to find that she was at least fifty-nine years old and was not visually appealing in any way to him. Because most men are visually motivated, this was quite a disappointment. The false expectations she set up initially had set her up for a fall! It's safe to say that she was definitely not what she portrayed herself to be!

Another time, a friend and I were at Starbucks when we noticed a very good-looking man pacing back and forth for at least twenty minutes outside. Eventually, an equally beautiful woman walked over to him. They immediately walked inside, sat next to us and began fighting.

She told him she only had fifteen minutes left to spend with him. He countered that she was thirty minutes late and that wasn't acceptable, then angrily stomped out. She in turn rushed angrily out the opposite door. They were both well dressed, he in a suit, she in a designer dress and high heels.

Once the woman was outside, she turned back towards him and hurriedly walked over in his direction and they began to fight horribly in the parking lot. They had met online and this was their first meeting. A man sitting next to us in the café looked at me and said, "Gives you good reason to say 'no' to online dating, wouldn't you say?" In the news today, it stated that online dating was on the decline. If the above example is an indication of a typical meeting, I can see why!

So if online dating isn't the best route, what is the next most obvious choice? Bars and dance clubs, right? Many people end up turning to bars and dance clubs to meet someone but come up empty there as well. So maybe you've gone to your local bar or dance club but can't meet the person that you would like to take home to mom.

Maybe they drink too much or they aren't faithful and are only looking for a one-night stand. On the latter, men generally fall into that category more than women, but I hear that the field is becoming competitive, with both sexes sharing equally in the "race." What about speed dating? I often wonder how much you can

actually learn about someone in the five minutes before the bell rings. Additional methods of meeting someone are the high paid dating services. However, many of those may be cost prohibitive to most of the general public and those that have been able to afford the services have stated the results were less than satisfactory and didn't yield much hope in the area of love.

The only place left, you may think, is at work. But, even at work, there may be the problem of a "no fraternization clause" prohibiting fellow employees from dating each other or you may feel that it could get too complicated should something go awry and you end the relationship. A very logical consequence of dating someone you work with or for.

So what do you do? Since the majority of your time is spent at work and the rest is usually at home, where do you go to meet someone and what do you do once you are there? Let me start by addressing the first part. There are a few easy places to meet someone that will say a lot about who they are. Primary among them is, believe it or not, the supermarket.

Fun Football Fact: On May 7th, 1982, a Los Angeles jury ruled against the NFL in an anti-trust suit brought by the Oakland Raiders and the Los Angeles Coliseum Commission. The verdict allowed the Oakland Raiders to move to Los Angeles.

The next time that you go to the grocery store, don't go in there with only speed in mind. Take your time to walk around a bit and check out each aisle. Take it leisurely, look around but don't troll, or someone might think you are odd. As you are walking up and down the aisles, get a good look at everything and everyone around you.

A good time to go would be between five and seven in the evening, when most single people do their shopping and married couples are either at home with each other or taking care of their children. While other times may be good as well, I have noticed in my area that this is when most of the single men and women are in the stores.

So, if you meet someone in the supermarket or somewhere else, how do you know if they are single? There is never a guarantee and a wedding ring or lack of one does not necessarily ensure anything. In a supermarket, however, you can usually tell by looking at what is in their cart. If the items in their cart (and this should be determined with some very casual, quick gazes, not long stares) seem to be meals for one or individual items, then there is a high potential that they are single. Again, however, there are no guarantees on this; their partner may simply be out of town. That is a question you will eventually need to ask them verbally.

So, how do you approach that someone who catches your eye while in the supermarket purchasing food? Most people are rushed and in a hurry, generally unaware of what is going on around them. So, you have to take the initiative. First, after you have quickly noticed what is in their basket, walk by them and smile. Hopefully, you will be passing the person, walking towards them. If not, you will have to try to strategically position yourself in another aisle for a more appropriate pass.

Fun Football Fact:
Amongst the original charter members of the NFL, which two teams remain? (Hint…one of the teams was already mentioned in this category on a previous Fun Football Fact.)

Once you have caught their eye with a smile and a slight nod, do more shopping but keep an eye out for the person you wish to start a conversation with. Perhaps, go to the end of the aisle and look at something there until you can find out where they are heading then head for that direction.

When you meet up again, smile again and say something like, "I have always loved that brand of peanut butter. It's smooth and creamy. I also love brand x but I can't always find it here." You get the idea. Make a comment about something in their basket. This, of course, assumes that you have already done your homework by checking out their basket. You can also try a less direct ploy by simply asking for help. In that case, try something like, "Do you happen to know which aisle the peanut butter is in?" Here, make sure that you don't ask about something that is already in that aisle!

If you are going to use the latter question, you may have to make another pass and bump into them again, this time laughing and using a more direct line like, "Seems like we keep bumping into each other. Maybe we should settle out of court." If you feel comfortable enough at that point, introduce yourself and ask for their name.

Fun Football Fact:
The Chicago Bears and the Arizona Cardinals are the only two charter members of the original National Football League still in existence.

If the person is receptive, give them a compliment and break the ice by joking about your groceries. Remember that laughter is always good. Once the ice is broken (and that can be one of your jokes if you are in the freezer section), say something like, "Since we have so much in common with groceries, perhaps you would like to join me for coffee or a hot cocoa sometime."

This will disarm them, perhaps bringing non-threatening images of home to mind if you ask them out for a cup of hot cocoa instead of just coffee. If they are interested, give them your cell phone number. Don't give your home phone number out to anyone that you don't know well at this point. Then say your goodbyes (unless, of course, you both continue to converse and are feeling comfortable) and thank them for making your grocery shopping trip a more enjoyable one.

Another potential meeting spot would be a local coffee shop. Bring your own coffee mug in, something that is interesting, could catch someone's eye and perhaps even be a much-needed conversation piece. (Some coffee shops give you a discount for brining in your own coffee mug. An additional benefit!) Grab a java and take a seat. Don't read the newspaper or a magazine as this will cover your face and give the signal that you don't wish to be disturbed. A good thing to do is to bring in some paperwork that doesn't unnecessarily disclose personal information such as your home address, home phone number or any financial information. Or bring in a pad of paper to do a bit of writing or drawing.

While you are working on your paperwork, jotting something on your pad or perhaps reading a small novel, look around and smile at the people you find attractive, attempting to catch a wandering eye. Once this has been accomplished, try to do so again and raise your mug to them the next time you do so.

If they smile back and give you an open posture response (this is where your knowledge of non-verbal communication will help you greatly), it may be your cue to step over to their table for a moment and start a conversation. This one can be a bit tricky as they may already be there with someone. In this case, you will need to wait a bit before you start engaging them in any type of conversation, even if it's with the eyes only, to ensure that they are alone or aren't with someone who appears to be more than just a friend or acquaintance. Once you get the nod of approval to come over and chat, go over to their table and give them a compliment, something like, "I was just noticing your smile and I was wondering if you would like to sit and chat over our cups of java?" See where it leads you from there.

Whatever you do, don't use what I call "pond scum" lines or you will instantly turn them away. Lines used upon first meeting such as: "Your eyes sparkle in the moonlight.", "What dazzling teeth you have." "You look incredible in that outfit and I thought I would say hello.", or the most stupid line of all, "What's your sign." If you use any of these lines as an opener, they are likely to tell you their "sign" is "exit" and they're leaving under it!

Another great place to meet people is at your local gym. Obviously, if you are both working out at a gym, you have at least one similar interest -- getting into or staying in shape. Notice the people around you and smile at them as they pass by.

If you see someone who strikes your fancy, approach them during one of their breaks and say "hi" on the way to your next set. For now, don't do anything more than simply saying "hi," unless he or she engages back. Try to make a point of going to the gym at the same time every day in order to increase your odds of running into

Fun Football Fact:
Which team was the first to win back-to-back Super Bowls?

Fun Football Fact:
The Green Bay Packers hold that honor, with two consecutive championships, in 1967 and 1968.

them again. As they begin to see you more at the gym, you will have a much better chance of striking up a real conversation. Once you have seen them at the gym a few times, go over (again on their down time) and say something like, "I love that exercise. It helps me build my biceps/forearms...." You can also ask what other exercises they like to do to help that body part and talk about what you like to do as well. The point is that by actually trying to exchange fitness ideas, that person will be more receptive. Whatever you do, don't mention off-limit areas and keep it to the non-personal body parts, such as arms, legs and abs.

The next time you see them, ask if perhaps they would like to work out sometime together and offer you cell phone number in case they do. Mention that it would be nice to have a spotting partner and that you would be more than willing to do the same for them. Don't take up too much of their time during the workout because, after all, that is what they are there for; they want to get or stay in shape and you don't want to wreck their "zone." A disclaimer for the gym -- it is NOT a meat market! Don't treat it as such. Be genuine in your approach.

Other great ways to meet singles would be by joining your local outdoor club (use the keywords "outdoor club - your city" and look one up on the Internet), a rock climbing gym, going to an auto parts store and browsing the isles, using the same technique as the grocer store, or by taking a social class at your local college. Some cities have chess café's where people go to play chess. Sign up for a cooking class or an auto mechanics course.

Look in your local newspaper for a variety of interesting options, including neighborhood picnics, fireman breakfasts, charity singles auctions (where dates with local men and women are auctioned off for charity), travel tours, public dances (ones not held in a bar or a pub, such as a beginner's square dance), charity events or even a beginners salsa dance night. For dances, make sure that it's not a "partner necessary" event by calling ahead.

Type in your Internet Browser: www.citysearch.com to find out the local happenings in your area. Another effective way to meet someone would be to volunteer for a charity, such as the *Special Olympics, Make-A-Wish Foundation, United Way* or *UNICEF*, to name a few. It's important to participate with sincerity, but you may also meet your soul mate there. You may find someone who will most likely have the same philanthropic views that you do.

Finally, while I don't know anyone who has participated in the Singles International Club, I have heard of it. Check out your local chapter (search the Internet for specifics) as they hold dances and picnics for singles to meet. They also have the Singles Travel International Club. This is just a short list of good meeting places to get the ball rolling. However, no matter which place you choose to go, remember that in all of your approaches it's best not to try to be "suave" or "debonair." Be yourself. Smile so that your eyes shine and be sincere. You will go much further if you behave in a kind manner than if you put on an act.

In a football game, "freezing" occurs when a player holds the ball for a long period of time without attempting to score points. You can't "freeze" if you want to participate in the game of love. You MUST forgo shyness. You will never make it onto the playing field until you do. There is nothing anyone can say or do, no magic potions or pills and no amount of coaching that will do this for you.

It may take work to build your confidence up, but one of the things that you have to remember is that "no" is just a word. While it may hurt your pride for a moment, try not taking it as anymore than that. If you let your fear of the word "no" get in the way, you will never be able to meet the partner of your dreams.

CHAPTER 18
Getting into the End Zone
Consistently—The Final Word

The point of football is to have the best strategy with consistent execution, so that you can make it to the end zone and score the most points, winning the game and eventually making it to the Super Bowl. As I pointed out before, the players have to memorize and fully understand the playbook in order to know the correct rules of engagement.

So let's take a brief look back at a few of the points we have discussed here so that you can keep winning points with the woman in your life one touchdown at a time! Since men are wired for speed, you need to learn to take time out for your relationship and not treat it as something you simply need to conquer. If you do, you will soon lose interest and try to move on to other things; and I guarantee you that your partner will move on to other things as well. *"Do you know that in a race all the runners compete, but only one receives the prize? So run that you may obtain it."* 1 Corinthians 9:24

What happens after a team wins the Super Bowl? Does everyone on the team call it a day and clear the locker room? No more practices? No more ballet lessons? (Yes many professional football players take ballet classes; it helps with their agility and coordination!) No more working out?

What most people don't see is the work done during the off season or how hard the players work to stay in shape so they can make it to the Super Bowl again the next year. In a relationship too, you must continually strive for the best.

If you want to make it to the Super Bowl year after year, you must persist in creating better moves and stronger plays, building your relationship muscles so that they are stronger and leaner. There is no magic liquid remedy to allow you to obtain the results you can only get from hard work and practice.

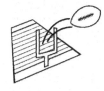

Fun Football Fact:
What quarterbacks were chosen for the NFL's 75th anniversary all-time greatest team?

Fun Football Fact:
The quarterbacks chosen for the NFL's 75th anniversary all-time greatest team were Sammy Baugh, Washington Redskins (1937-52); Otto Graham, Cleveland Browns (1946-55); Joe Montana, San Francisco 49ers (1979-92), Kansas City Chiefs (1993 - 94); and Johnny Unitas, Baltimore Colts (1956-72), San Diego Chargers (1973).

No one can make your love grow other than you and your partner. That's why you must strive to keep your relationship fresh, spontaneous and filled with life. If you do this, the end result will be a dedication and love that is incredibly fulfilling for both of you. The reason so many relationships and marriages fail is because one or more of the partners does not put in the time, effort or work that is required to make it thrive. Remember you are a team when you are in a relationship. In order to stay on the team, you need to invest time with the other player.

Fun Football Fact:
Who holds the career record for most interceptions?

To date, there are only three players in NFL history who have scored six touchdowns in a single game: Ernie Nevers (November 28, 1929), Dub Jones (November 25, 1951) and Gale Sayers (December 12, 1965). They are an elite group. But, how did they get to be the best? By investing a lot of time honing their skills and by putting all of their energy into their game. They focused and did the work.

In order to be in a relationship that not only survives the test of time, but also thrives, flourishes and grows, you must become part of such an elite group, doing the work, focusing on your relationship and honoring your partner. Remember what I said in the first chapter? "One of the most valuable lessons you can learn is that once your mate is satisfied, you will be in for the game of your life as she will want to show her appreciation and satisfy you!"

What I have said throughout this book is that in order for a woman to be truly interested in rocking your world in every way, she needs to feel that you are connected. She needs relational intimacy (remember that this is NOT sexual intimacy).

Fun Football Fact:
Paul Krause holds the career record for most interceptions with a total of eighty-one.

While you are tactile, women are geared more for emotional nurturing. An important note for both men and women to remember and NOT forget is that each partner needs to feel he/she is emotional safe with you and able to share anything without judgment or future reproach. *"Everyone should be quick to listen, slow to speak and slow to become angry." James 1:19*

There are three main ingredients that are required to make it to the Super Bowl of relationships and beyond: you must do your best, be prepared and never give up. So, jump onto the field of love with the faith that all things are possible if you work hard and believe in yourself. *"Love is patient and kind; love is not jealous or boastful; it is not arrogant or rude. Love does not insist on its own way; it is not irritable or resentful; it does not rejoice at wrong, but rejoices in the right. Love bears all things, believes all things, hopes all things, endures all things. Love never ends." 1 Corinthians 13:4-8*

And on that note, I'm off to the playing field of love!

The Final Fun Football Facts

Fun Football Fact:
Who owns the NFL - the organization, not the individual franchises?

Fun Football Fact Answer:
This is a complex question. NFL Enterprises is a limited partnership executed under the laws of the State of Delaware. They are in the business of exhibiting football games.

Fun Football Fact:
How many conferences are there in the NFL?

Fun Football Fact Answer:
There are two: the American Football Conference and the National Football Conference.

Fun Football Fact:
Which team most recently won back-to-back Super Bowls?

Fun Football Fact Answer:
The Denver Broncos won it in 1998 and 1999.

Fun Football Fact:
Which team has won the most Super Bowls?

Fun Football Fact Answer:
The San Francisco 49ers have won a total of five Super Bowls: 1982, 1985, 1989, 1990, and 1995.
(***Dallas has also won 5)

CHAPTER 19
Relationship Advice from Legendary
NFL Clutch-Kickers

Garo Yepremian

Garo Yepremian NFL and Vital Statistics

Position: Place Kicker for the Miami Dolphins, Detroit Lions, New Orleans Saints and The Tampa Bay Buccaneers.
Career Span: 1966 - 1981
Height/Weight at the beginning of his career: 5'8" 142 lbs
Height/Weight as his career progressed: 5'8', 175 lbs
Two of his most famous seasons: 1971 and "1972 Perfect Season" (Miami Dolphins)
Born in: Lamaca, Cyprus (Garo moved to the U.S. when he was 22)
Date of birth: June 2, 1944
Married: Maritza Javian (maiden) now Maritza Yepremian on June 12, 1971, 10 days after Garo's 27th birthday.
Career Highs: Known as the kicker who ended the "longest game" in NFL history as well as one of the premier place kickers of all time.
Career Insiders Information: Garo is a left-footed place kicker whose career spanned 15 years in the NFL. In 177 games, he converted 210 out of 313 field goal attempts and 1,074 points. To date, Garo still holds the record for the "all-time leading scorer" for the Miami Dolphins with 830 points. Additionally, he holds quite a number of team kicking records including scoring 110 consecutive points after a touchdown.

Fun Football Fact:
What year is Garo Yepremian known for ending the "longest game" in NFL history and which teams were playing?

Garo Yepremian NFL Career Beginnings

If I were making a guess, I would doubt there was ever a more interesting start in NFL history then that of Garo Yepremian. Garo Yepremian was born in Lamaca, Cyprus with very humble beginnings. In fact, he did not grow up dreaming of becoming a football legend, let alone a hero or a star, but rather he dreamed of going to college, marrying the right woman and having a family.

Things changed dramatically when at age 22, Garo's brother, who happened to be attending Indiana University, observed a man kicking a ball soccer style and he thought it was a novelty. Overhearing the people around him bragging about the kicker and how great he was, Garo's brother called him and said, "Garo, you have the strongest legs on the island of Cyprus. If you come to the United States and kick a football you can get a free education."

That was all it took for Garo, because without hesitation, he boarded a plane with a dream and a hope of becoming a soccer player in the U.S. Little did he know he was going to be playing football, a game he had never seen before. Not speaking any English, Garo quickly found that it wasn't as easy to get into college as his brother made it sound. Yet with dreams still in tact, and a mere six weeks after landing in America, incredibly Garo turned his expectations to the NFL.

A major event occurred when on Wednesday, October 12th, 1966, Garo headed to the Atlanta Falcons Camp for try outs. The following day, October 13th, he found himself at the Detroit Lions Camp, and lo and behold he was signed that very evening. Soon after, the Detroit Lions discovered that Garo didn't even have a working permit, yet by Friday, October 14, 1966, the Detroit Lions and Garo Yepremian did what normally takes a year to do; they obtained a work permit! A full day was spent in handling all the details at the immigration office, the social security office and the police station. By Saturday, October 15th, Garo was on a plane heading to Baltimore where he began his career in the NFL. On Sunday, October 16, 1966, Garo Yepremian played his very first game against the Baltimore Colts. Did I happen to mention that it was also the very first game Garo had ever seen? What a week that turned out for Garo! Here is Garo's account of that fateful game:

"On the Sunday after I arrived in Baltimore, I played my first game. I didn't even know how to put on my uniform! As I was watching the other players, I noticed that one of them was taping their ankle. I thought I should tape my left arm because I wouldn't

124

be using it much, so I proceeded to apply layers of tape. Noticing what I was doing, one of the players came over to ask me why I was taping my arm. As he helped me peel the tape off, which of course ripped off all the hair on my arm, he informed me that only ankles got taped. The other players and locker room staff observed that I didn't know what I was doing when it came to putting on a uniform so they began to help me. While I was being helped into my uniform, one of the players told me that the game we were about to play was 'very very dangerous.' He also advised me to run out as soon as I kicked the ball because, as he put it, 'they're gonna kill you.' I thought he was putting me on. Once the uniform was on, they placed the helmet on my head. I couldn't stand the face guard, so I wound up playing the entire season without a facemask. As we went onto the field the coach called me and said that we had lost the coin toss and that I had to kick off.

I got the ball and placed it on the designated tee at the 40-yard line (it was 40 at that time). The coach told me to wait for the ref to blow the whistle and then I could kick off. As I waited for the whistle, I lined up to kick off. At that moment, I heard the head coach yelling from the sidelines. 'Garo, as soon as you kick the ball come stand by me.' I thought to myself, 'Oh my goodness! They weren't lying to me! They're gonna kill me. I wonder if I'm making enough money for this job.' But I didn't have much time to contemplate the enormity of the situation because the referee blew the whistle and I ran towards the ball, took a swing and had a perfect kick!

It was the most beautiful sight watching the ball going end over end. To tell the truth it was such a great kick that I forgot all about running out as I had been instructed to do, but instead stood there admiring my work. A moment or two later it dawned on me that I had kicked off, and since they were paying me quite a bit of money, perhaps I should be kind enough and pick up the tee.

As I bent over to pick it up, I heard a bunch of loud footsteps behind me. All of a sudden I remembered that I had been warned to get off the field and get out of there before I was killed. I forgot the tee and just thought about saving my life!

So I ran towards the sidelines as the coach had instructed me, and as I did, I glanced over my shoulder to see what was happening. It was then that I noticed four very large Baltimore Colt players catching up to me. I picked up speed, running as fast as I could in order to save my life. I ran so fast that I passed the sidelines. The next thing I saw was the bench, so feeling relieved and certain I would be safe, I sat down. As I took a breath, I heard the biggest roar I had ever heard in my life coming from the crowd. I looked up to see what had happened and would you believe I realized that I was on the wrong bench! I was sitting on the Baltimore Colts bench! And so, that's I how I started my career, which spanned 15 years."

A Personal Glimpse into Garo Yepremian's Marriage: Advice from a Pro

Fun Football Fact: On December 25, 1971 Garo kicked a 37 yard field goal, which ended the "longest game" in NFL history. What teams were part of this NFL historic moment? The Miami Dolphins against the Kansas City Chiefs.

The game lasted 82 minutes, 40 seconds when Garo ended the game in sudden-death overtime in an AFC Divisional Playoff Game.

In December of 1970 Garo Yepremian met the love of his life, the woman who also became his life partner. Her name at the time was Maritza Javian. By the third date, Garo knew that she was going to be his wife and he told her of his prediction. She laughed, but he proposed anyway and she accepted. On June 12, 1971, Maritza Javian became Maritza Yepremian and they have since been happily married for 34 years. They've also been blessed with two wonderful sons.

Like most marriages there have been ups and downs, but there has been much more laughter and joy, than there has been tears that were cried together. Garo and his wife Maritza have a strong faith in God and often pray together. Garo said: "God has tested us many times and we hope we have passed the test." In 1989 Maritza was diagnosed with breast cancer. It was a shocking and vulnerable time for Garo and Maritza as well as their two sons. They were devastated by the news and scared to death. Garo said, "My sons were young and as their father I had to provide personal strength. It was my job to stay relaxed, yet focused, because I had to assure them that everything would be okay. The only problem was that I had my own internal conflict because I wasn't sure what would happen or that everything would be okay."

Fortunately for his family, Maritza not only survived the breast cancer, but she thrived. She had a lumpectomy and radiation therapy and the doctors gave her a 90% cure rate. But nine years later, the cancer came back. Only this time it came back much more aggressively. Garo and Maritza did what they had always done in their marriage, which was to communicate with each other and pray to God. After much thoughtful consideration, they talked it over and decided that the best treatment was to have a mastectomy on both breasts. Garo stated: "Thank God things are going great now and the doctor only has Maritza come in for a check up once a year versus every six months. We're very grateful."

Garo and Maritza believe that marriage is a partnership. Quoting Garo: "To succeed in marriage you must be partners in everything you do. During Maritza's breast cancer, I felt her pain and her thoughts, and we just kept communicating. In fact, there hasn't been a time in our lives that we don't stay in close communication. My wife has never opened her eyes in the morning without first saying I love you. And I always say the same words back to her. When I leave home for a trip that she's not able to attend, I always find notes in my jacket pocket, suitcase or shaving kit telling me how much she's going to miss me. She always says, 'God keep you safe and bring you back to me. I can't wait until you get home. And I can't wait to get home because this is my home, my comfort zone, my family, and my life. My wife is the love of my life and so are my kids. My children are 29 and 31 and we are a very close-knit family. We speak at least two or three times a day and my sons come over for dinner at least two times a week. One of the best pieces of advice I can give to anyone, is that family is of the utmost importance above anything else."

Fun Football Fact:
What is the only season that Garo Yepremian missed during his 15 year NFL history and why?

Garo does not like to be apart from his wife and feels that closeness is very important. "I take my wife wherever I go if I can. I do a lot of charity work, including golf tournaments. If a golf tournament invites me and they don't invite my wife, I won't go. If I were to go by myself, where would my marriage be? I don't want to be separated from the woman I love."

With a sterling wisdom that can only come from one who has been where we all want to be in our relationships, Garo has the following to say:

"I would also give couples another piece of advice which is very important and that is to always say I'm sorry. When my wife and I argue or have disagreements, we have never ever thought of divorce. Not even one time. We wouldn't even joke about. When we argue, one of us usually comes back and says, 'I am sorry' and we iron out things."

One last piece of advice from Garo is something he would tell his own children in regards to love, commitment and marriage: "If you're making a commitment to marry someone, you have to be 100% sure of your love for them and theirs love for you. There should be no questions before you start your life together. I have seen far too many people start their married life wondering who makes more money, which one is going to take what if they separate and other ridiculous thoughts like that. It is not a good way to start off a marriage with those types of thoughts. That will only lead to a bad situation. Be sure you both have the same feelings for each other before you get married and remember that it's a commitment you are making for life."

Although Garo has made two Super Bowl appearances in his history at the NFL and has set numerous records, his life is very full today with other important things. What is he doing with his life now? Garo Yepremian has founded the Garo Yepremian foundation, www.garoyepremianfoundation.org, which donates money to the research of brain tumors in the hopes of a cure.

Fun Football Fact:
Garo missed the 1969 season when he proudly volunteered to serve in the U.S. Army.

His commitment to this charity and helping others excel has always been a passionate part of his life, but his focus changed dramatically when both his wife and his daughter-in-law were diagnosed with cancer. It was at that time that he focused his charitable influence onto research in the field of cancer.

A few years ago his son had been seriously dating a woman whose name was Debby Lu for four years when she was diagnosed with an inoperable and fatal brain tumor. A short time later, Garo's son Azad proposed to her. His son vowed to Debby Lu that he would marry her and they would fight the tumor together. The doctors gave her six months to live. Yet, Garo's son married her and took care of her for six years before she succumbed to her brain tumor. During that time, Azad was always positive and upbeat with Debby Lu. This gave her the strength to carry that same lighted fire within herself.

What greater testament to the values Garo and Maritza have passed on to their children then that kind of commitment and love? Garo is certain, and I am too, that his son's love increased the length and quality of her life. Because of that experience, Garo now does beautiful works of art by painting with oil. Following along the lines of his life message of community outreach, he donates most of the proceeds from the sale of his paintings to brain tumor research.

As a highly sought after motivational speaker, Garo also participates in golf tournaments. He is a spokesman for Fonar, which makes the only upright open MRI. Garo also holds his own golf tournament every June and a banquet every September. He has chaired and is involved in many national charitable foundations, and is actively involved in numerous charity organizations.

With all that he has accomplished in his life, the most important success he feels he has achieved is that of being a husband and a father. What an admirable and honorable man. My hat is off to you Garo!

Don Cockroft

Don Cockroft NFL and Vital Statistics

Position: Kicker for the Cleveland Browns
Career Span: 1967 - 1980
Height / Weight: 6'1" 195 lbs
Married: Barbara Jo Ewing on August 12, 2000.
Career Highs: Known as the greatest and most famous punter in ASC history. His Number "0" jersey is one of only three retired numbers at Adams State College. Don was inducted into Adams State College Football Hall of Fame on September 21, 2000 and the Cleveland Sports Hall of Fame in June of 2002. On October 29, 1972, he kicked a 57-yard field goal for the Cleveland Browns.

Career Insider Information: Don is known for being one of the greatest clutch kickers in NFL history as well as one of the nation's greatest college kickers and punters of all time. He was the last true full-time double duty kicker in the NFL as both a punter and kicker. When Don was drafted by the Cleveland Browns, he had some pretty tall shoes to fill, that of the legendary kicker Lou Groza and he did so with celebrated skill. Don established himself as one of the most valuable offensive weapons the Cleveland Browns ever had.

Don Cockroft NFL Career Beginnings

Don Cockroft began playing the game of football in his younger years while living on a farm in Delta Colorado. With the encouragement of his Dad and four brothers, the spirited young boy grew to love football as his father did. Being a naturally gifted athlete, any and all sports were of interest to him and he indulged in them by playing just about any sport that was put in his path, basketball being his favorite. The passion he displayed for sports and the dedication he gave to them would help pave the path for his future as a world renowned NFL player.

In 7th grade, Don suited up for football for the very first time. As he put on his cleats, he observed the very large 3" metal spikes in his shoes and said to himself, "Holy cow! If anyone steps on me with these cleats, they're gonna put a hole in my body! They look dangerous!" This was one of his first impressions of football and he continued the game through the rest of Junior High and High School, being voted Outstanding Athlete in his senior year.

Fun Football Fact: How many field goals and extra points did Don Cockroft score in his 13 year history in the NFL?

Once Don graduated from Fountain-Fort Carson High School in Fountain, Colorado, he headed off to Adams State College in Alamosa, Colorado where he earned a degree in Secondary Education with majors in Biology & Physical Education. Thinking a career in the NFL was impossible for a little country boy like him, his scholastic goals were to earn a teaching degree and also coach. At the beginning of his college career, Don never considered becoming a professional player in the NFL. However, fate would intervene and it was during his junior year in college that the world of football began to stand up and take real notice of this exceptional athlete and he became a highly sought after draft pick for many of the top teams in the NFL.

When interviewing Don, he revealed that while he was in college, he had been selected to play in both the North-South Shrine Game and the All-Star Game in Chicago, IL, with "the big boys." He considers that to be one of the greatest honors and privileges of his sports career and he believes it was because of his success in the North-South Shrine Game that the path of his life changed forever. It was at that time the Cleveland Browns drafted him. Here's Don's story:

"The Browns called me while I was in Chicago, the night before the 1967 NFL draft, and they told me they were thinking of drafting me fairly high. This was the first year of common draft, which meant only one team was allowed to draft you. They asked me if I would play for the Browns if drafted and I said of course! As soon as I hung up the phone I rushed around looking for a map of the U.S. in order to find out where Ohio was. I thought 'Man that's a long way from Colorado!' Before the All-Star game, I had never been any further north than Nebraska and that only was by car. I had never even been on an airplane." As I continued to interview Don, he shared with me a funny story he experienced during his time in the NFL. Here it is in his words:

"One of the most embarrassing, as well as rushed football moments in my life took place when I played in the College All-Star game in Chicago and the following day, I had to play my first game with the Cleveland Browns. I was brought on as the heir to the greatest kicker of all time, Lou "the toe" Groza. Due to tight scheduling, I went straight from the airport to my first Browns game. I had never met any of my teammates, so this game was my first chance to interact with them. During the pre-game warm up at the goal post I met Lou 'the toe' Groza and attempted to strike up a conversation with him. I said, 'Mr. Groza, it's really tough to miss these extra points.'

At that time, extra points amounted to a 10 yard kick because the goal post was positioned on the goal line. Lou was not in a talkative mood, and simply said, 'Yes son, it's kind of hard to miss them, but you do miss them on occasion.' Lou had only missed a hand full of extra points in his 21 year career.

When the game started, I was called on the field to kick my first extra point for Cleveland. I was very nervous and I could have sworn the grass was at least four inches high. I also knew that the Browns were testing me to find out what the 'rookie' could do. As I stood there prepared to make my first kick for the team, my nerves were frayed and I not only missed the kick, but it didn't even come close. When I left the field to go to the bench, Mr. Groza met me on the sideline, smiling ear to ear and said, 'Well, you can miss 'em son, you can miss 'em!' I call that my 'perfect onside kick' which didn't come close to making it!"

As stated earlier, Don had a passion for sports and in that passion, he had an insatiable appetite for learning all he could to enhance his own performance. "Throughout my time in the NFL, I always enjoyed studying other kickers and their styles. During the day, Ray Guy, who punted for the Raiders, was known as one of the best punters in NFL history. One day I decided I was going to watch Ray punt. I noticed that Ray would swing his leg to warm up and I said to myself, 'Man I don't do that! Maybe I will try it to that tomorrow before I punt.'

The following day, during the Browns game against the Bengals in Cincinnati, thinking I would improve my punting, I tried the warm-up as I had witnessed Ray Guy doing the previous day. As I gracefully swung my leg high in the air for warm-up, I slipped and fell on my behind. Embarrassed, I thought to myself, 'If I get up quickly, don't make much commotion and act like nothing happened, no one is going to see this and it will go unnoticed.' I was not prepared for what happened next and I certainly did not anticipate such a response, but as I stood, I witnessed 63,000 Cincinnati Bengals fans giving me a standing ovation for my obviously wonderful coordination. That was definitely one of my most embarrassing moments!

Fun Football Fact: Don Cockroft scored 1,080 points, 216 field goals and 432 extra points in his 13-year history in the NFL. He is second only to the legendary Lou Groza for team records.

Another embarrassing moment occurred when I ran onto the field without my helmet on and the officials were waving their arms at me. As I watched them, I began to think, 'Man! I haven't even made the kick yet!' It wasn't until the referee began to point at his head that I realized I had forgotten to put on my helmet. And you can't get in the game without a helmet. When asked to speak about my Christian faith, I use this story as an illustration and I quote passages from Ephesians 6 about the Armor of God. The correlation is that as a Christian we must put on the Helmet of Salvation. You can't get into the game of life without it."

With a spectacular career in the NFL that spanned over 13 years, it's no wonder Don has so many wonderful and historic memories to share with us. However, there was a specific time during his NFL career that was a defining moment for him. It was one that was so full of impact, that to do this day, he still uses the examples as a platform to help people who want to give in and give up to those around them who are blocking their way. Read on as Don shares his powerful story:

"One of the most memorable times in my 25 years of athletic competition, was during one particular game in which I experienced my very worst and my all-time greatest moments. It happened during my fifth year as a kicker for the Browns. Prior to beginning that year, I had been praying to determine if I was supposed to continue in football. In searching for God's will in my life, I was led to *Luke 9:23* where Christ says, *'If you want to follow after me you must deny yourself, take up your cross daily and stay close to me.'* Though I was using my football career to honor God, the question was, 'are you willing to deny yourself (give up football) to follow Christ.' It was early that year, long before training camp, that I bowed before God and said, 'Lord I will do what you want me to do, just show me your path.' No other path was open to me at that time, so I went to the Brown's training camp that year, not sure what my future held, but totally confident that God held my future. Looking for signs from God as to my direction in life, that summer before the season began, I received a phone call from the Billy Graham Crusade.

They asked if I would share my testimony during a Billy Graham Crusade to be held at the Cleveland stadium that fall. My thought when I received the call was, if my career is over, there would be no better way to leave Cleveland than to stand on the same football field where I had kicked for five years and share my faith in Jesus Christ. I shared with 40,000 people attending the crusade that night, 'the most important thing in life is that Christ has control of your life.'

It turned out that my career wasn't over. I was kicking so well, that the draftee who was to replace me didn't have a chance. I was having by far my best year as a punter/kicker for the Browns. One particular game stood out that year for me and it was the 10th game of the season. We were playing our arch rivals the Pittsburg Steelers. It was a cold, rainy, nasty, muddy; very typical November in Cleveland. It was an extremely critical game for the Browns. If we won the game we were tied with Pittsburgh. If we lost we were two games down with only four games to go.

As the game progressed, we were ahead of Pittsburg 20-3 at half time. I had already kicked two field goals in the first half. During the second half and I think on the second play from scrimmage, Franko Harris ran 75 yards untouched and Pittsburgh scored early in the second half. Now the score was 20-10 and I kicked my third field goal. At that point, Pittsburg scored again. We were up with five minutes left in the game and they scored a touchdown making it 23-24. My teammates and I were praying that Mike Phipps would score a touchdown. With 2 minutes and 5 seconds remaining on the clock, the Browns drive for a score stalled at the 20-yard line and I was sent out to kick a 27-yard chip shot to win the game.

As I lined up to make the kick, I experienced the worst moment in my athletic career as the ball flew through the air and missed by one inch to the right. Literally 83,000 fans sat in stunned silence and I stood in shock. I thought to myself, 'I'm having a phenomenal, nearly All-Pro year and I missed the most important kick of my life! God why would you allow this to happen?' I couldn't believe it! I even told God, 'You could have moved the goal post three inches and I would have made it!' After the missed kick, I dejectedly headed over to the bench where one of my teammates was cussing me out, but through his words I only remember asking God, 'Why! Why! Why!'

The answer was that God didn't miss the kick, I did. I disobeyed one of most important rules in kicking, which is when you kick the field goal keep your head down, keep your eye on the football and do not look up. I looked up during that kick because I wanted to see it go through the uprights like everyone else, and in doing so; I pulled my body off balance, pushing it to the right by one inch. When I got back to the bench my whole life was flashing before my eyes. There was one teammate who encouraged me; it was my Christian Brother Billy Andrews who was a Linebacker. He was the first guy to come over, throw his arm around me and say, 'Keep your chin up! Were gonna get the ball back and you're gonna get a second chance.'

Pittsburg in the meantime had the ball and our defense was stopping them cold. As the seconds ticked away and Pittsburg punted back to the Browns, I prayed, 'Lord please give me a second chance, I'll keep my head down, please give me a second chance.' In a matter of seconds, with two unbelievable pass completions, I was awarded a second chance with 13 seconds remaining on the clock.

What's so amazing is that this field goal was only inches away from where I missed the infamous field goal only moments earlier. As I lined up, my heart was beating quickly. This time I obeyed the rules of kicking. I relaxed, took a step, kicked through the ball and kept my head down the entire time. When my foot hit the ball, I knew it was good! When I finally looked up, the ball had sailed dead center through the uprights and we won 26-24!

The lessons I had spent a life time learning and adhering too about never quitting or giving up, had a powerful impact during that game. God is the author of second chances in life and I didn't give up on the game that day. It's easy in life to give up and quit when there are so many who will try to discourage you. We need to preserve, keeping our eye on God and never give up. Rewards unseen. For me, the missed field goal that day became a reward unseen. In the city of Cleveland it is still considered one of the greatest games ever played."

Highlights of Don's Career

· 1972: All-Pro Punter/Received the NFL Golden Toe Award/ Colorado's Outstanding Pro Athlete

· Longest Punt/71 yards-twice/Longest field goal-57 Yards/ Kicked five field goals in one game
· Retired from Browns in 1981as the 8th Leading Scorer in NFL History with 1080 points

· Noted as a one of the greatest clutch kickers in NFL/ Made 17 of 17 kicks in game winning situations

· Inducted into the Cleveland Sports Hall of Fame in June of 2002

A Personal Glimpse with Don and Barb Cockroft: Advice from a Pro and a Pro's Life Partner

"I think that it's really important for two people in a relationship to have a similar faith in God and hopefully a lot in common in other areas as well. There's got to be a lot of common ground to really make a relationship work. Without question, if a couple prays together it helps to bind them together. I think that taking the time to pray together and read God's word every day is an important part of a healthy relationship. Money matters are critical to the success of a partnership as well. Similarities in spending and saving can be life or death to a relationship. It's crucial that a couple agrees on financial matters beforehand and understands the financial aspects of a relationship.

Couples and people in general, need to know that a person won't change overnight and in many cases the older we get the more set we are in our ways. Communication is vitally important if a relationship is going to last. That is the most valuable thing a couple can do. I would also emphasize listening. Becoming a good listener is important to a good relationship.

We must also do everything possible to make sure the romance thrives. That same romantic feeling you had when you were dating, when you became engaged, and when you first got married...the sparks. You can create romance by doing the things you both love and have in common together. And to avoid arguments, resolve them immediately by communicating. Trust is vital to a relationship. I admit that I still have a long way to go in regards to this issue."

Barb's Relationship Advice—Pearls of Wisdom

"The number one thing I believe is that you should know how your partner celebrates holidays. Make sure your lifestyles are the same and that you compliment each other in that arena. Go through a whole calendar year and celebrate the holidays prior to getting married. Get to know the family you are marrying into because you are marrying the family and not just the man.

You need to make each other number one. If you're tired of playing second fiddle, consider where that second instrument came from that has replaced you. I totally believe you must have a firm belief in God and share that commitment together. When your relationship hits rocky times, which every relationship will, you have to believe in God and put your trust in Him because there are certain things in life you can't handle alone."

Don and Barb have six children combined and two grandchildren.

What Is Don Doing Now?

Don is currently in the mortgage business as a loan specialist dealing with residential financing. He is also a highly sought after motivational speaker. If you would like to book Don for a speaking engagement please contact him at: dcockroft12@yahoo.com

Nick Lowery

Nick Lowery NFL and Vital Statistics

Position: Kicker for the Kansas City Chiefs and the New York Jets.
Career Span: 1980 - 1997
Date of birth: May 27th
Career Highs: Broke his Idol Jan Stenerud's NFL career field goal record. Nick is known as the most accurate Kicker in NFL history from 1980 - 1997.
Career Insider Information: 8 teams cut Nick 11 times before he made it to the Pros. Once there, he set quite a few records in the NFL. His motto is "persistence and never giving up" and he is often asked to do motivational speaking on the subject. "Overcome great odds to achieve truly lasting success...on the field and beyond."

Nick Lowery was always a talented, extremely coordinated and ambitious athlete who set his sights on a football career at a very early age. Once graduating from High School, Nick attended Dartmouth where he earned a BA in Government with a minor in Drama. During that time, he was a legislative Aid in the US Senate before making it to the NFL. He is in fact the first pro athlete to graduate with a Masters Degree from Harvard's Kennedy School of Government.

Fun Football Fact:
What year did Nick Lowery break the record for the most field goals by his idol Jan Stenerud?
Nick Lowery NFL Career Beginnings

Some Important Highlights and Poignant Times of Nicks Career

· Certainly breaking all time record for most Field Goals against Jacksonville in 1996, and kicking the last playoff game winner in Arrowhead Stadium.

· Bringing my parents to the NFL Pro Bowl in Hawaii was an all time favorite. Seeing them up in the stands during games...

- Playing with Marcus Allen and Joe Montana in 1994 and making it to the AFC Championship game was really cool. Leading the NFL in scoring in 1990. Being on David Letterman twice with the NY Jets - kicking field goals outside on 53rd street the first year in 1994 and in the studio in 1995!

- Beating out Jan Stenerud, the only pure kicker in the NFL Hall of Fame and shattering all of his records.

- Aunt Margaret had cerebral palsy, yet became a professional writer and university educated librarian at the University of Utah. When 'Kick with Nick for Cerebral Palsy' won the National UCP award in 1989, it became the longest running player fundraising program in the history of the NFL. It raised almost a million $$ and educated people on the rights of the disabled. So when I hosted the UCP telethon and was able to have Aunt Margaret on as a guest, I witnessed her ability to passionately and calmly present herself. It was one of the most moving times of my life.

Fun Football Fact:
Nick Lowery broke Jan Stenerud's record of 373 field goals on October 13, 1996. How many did Nick score? A record setting 383!

- Getting a personally written letter from Bill Clinton on the President's own White House stationery after kicking 5 field goals and all the Chiefs Points in the 1993 Monday Night Football showdown between Joe Montana and John Elway - which prevented me from being at the Rose Garden Ceremony signing off the Americorps Bill, which I worked on in the White House Office of National Service earlier that Winter and Spring. It was President Clinton's first major piece of legislation.

- Setting the NFL record for field goal accuracy (80.4%), raising it from near 70% to a whole new plateau.

- Nick Lowery converted a Chiefs single-season record four field goals from 50 yards or beyond in 1980 and converted a Chiefs single game record two 50-yard field goals on three separate occasions.

A Personal Glimpse into Nick Lowery's Life

In addition to Nick's 17 years of NFL achievements, he also sets an example off the field, raising money and awareness for worthy causes. One of his important achievements was founding *"Adult Role Models For Youth - ARMY"* (with the YMCA). In addition, he headed up Kansas City's America's Promise Drive, producing 900 pledges from the city's corporate, nonprofit and private communities. On September 8, 2000, General Colin Powell celebrated America's Promise Drive as the foremost metropolitan effort in the country. He also won the National UCP award in 1989 for the 'Kick with Nick for Cerebral Palsy.'

Nick Lowery is the only American to work for President Reagan in regard to the Drug Abuse Policy, in addition to working for both President Bush and President Clinton in the White House Office of National Service. His *Adult Role Models for Youth (ARMY) Program* (now known as *Youthfriends - youthfriends.org*) used high profile mentors such as professional athletes to engage more citizens in regular mentoring relationships with inner-city youth in Kansas City. The International YMCA recognized the program in 1992. In 1995, Nick was approached by Johns Hopkins Center for American Indian Health requesting he apply his urban-youth ARMY program to reach native youth and families. With the help of the NFL Players Association, Native Vision, a sports and life skills program, has reached thousands of American Indian youth from over 30 tribes for more than 8 years. Native Vision *(nativevision.org)* was recognized on ABC's Oprah as the best new program for Native Youth In 1997.

Besides being a very giving and strong influence, Nick writes poetry. Here's a poem he wrote entitled:

Love Asks

For love asks not the ill timed question,
But rather
Soaks the soul
In loving lather
Cleanses rather
And forgets hurts
Embracing you and
With profound compassion,
Revealing underneath

True and timeless passion
For all the world has known
That love endured
Is truth shown
And life preferred

Nick on Handling Situations

"I was competing against my former idol, the legendary Jan Stenerud, (the only pure kicker in the NFL Hall of Fame) in training camp and it was getting very close to decision time. My teammates were all very close to Jan partly because he was a father figure and mostly because he was the last player to play in the Super Bowl won ten years earlier. I knew I was getting close to winning the job because when I went back to my dorm room at Eaton Hall after a long, hot day and two practices, I pulled up the sheets and there in my bed and my wardrobe were five feet of beautifully and evenly spread, smooth, warm, wormy, pungent cow manure! I knew if they had to resort to those tactics I must be getting close to replacing Jan!"

Fun Football Fact:
What record did Nick break that involved two field goals and 50 yards?

"Once while we were playing the SD Chargers, I pulled my groin a few weeks earlier (radio stations had been making jokes about how I had 'pulled my groin') and I was on the sidelines on a rather cold night. I wanted to make sure I didn't pull it again so I crouched in front of the heater on the sidelines for a few seconds and one of my teammates alerted me to the fact that it had burned a hole in my pants! Rather than run out to the field with a big hole in my pants, the equipment manager, Mike Davidson, stitched up the six-inch hole with laces. I ran out at the end of game thusly repaired and ended up kicking the 300th goal of my career, plus I was the game winner with less than one minute left. We beat the Chargers, 16-14."

Fun Football Fact:
Nick Lowery became the first player in NFL history to convert two field goals from beyond 50 yards in a single game on multiple occasions.

A Question Nick Is Often Asked

"One question I am often asked in my career is do I have any superstitions. My response is of course not ~ other than I burn incense and pour the blood of a chicken over my head every game. Other than that, no superstitions." (I'm only joking!)

Nick Lowery: Advice from a Pro

"Certainly when it comes to relationships this is not a science as much as it is an art! There is no more difficult or complex illusion than to think one can have control in relationships. For example - when we talk about healthy psychology on the Headgames Radio show with Dr Andrew Jacobs and Dr John Eliot (both performance psychologists) and Peter Roby, Director of the Center for the Study of Sport in Society, we talk about focusing only on my actions and interpretations- not the 11 people weighing 3000 pounds who are paid millions of $$ to block my kick if not kill me! I can control how I prepare and anticipate kicking the ball, but I can't control the crowds. I can control how I approach each game and kick through, which is my preparation and I can control my focus and discipline.

By contrast, the illusion of control is far more difficult in relationships because when you love someone you bring them into your most intimate psychological circle. The conundrum is that as much as you love them and care about them you can't control them! You can only stay true to who you are and stay clear about how you feel about them. You cannot control what they do, or who they are. Most people when defining a relationship spend much of their time defining it by how the other makes them feel!

They talk about how someone did something to them or how someone made them feel, when in reality you can only choose how you interpret everything that happens to you - every thought that you put in your head, and hence, every feeling that stems from those thoughts. Wayne Dyer's original ground breaking book, 'Your Erroneous Zones' talks about this. The challenge is the most difficult in relationships because when you love someone it's hard to separate your own feelings about that person from their behavior. It's sort of the reverse of what we do with children: We say "your behavior is bad,' but it's not healthy to say to children, 'Since your behavior is bad, YOU are bad.'

"To my way of thinking here's the key: In relationships, it is important to LINK behavior to feelings or we end up coupled with people we love who are BAD for us!! Just because we love someone, and just because they love us, does NOT mean that they are good for us, or that we are good for each other!

My philosophy and basic healthy psychology is that we can only take care of what we can control - we cannot control others, even those we love who are "committed" to us. Keep things simple and don't worry about the things we can't control - i.e. other people and their actions!! Abraham Maslow's, Self-Actualization, a fundamental contribution to modern psychology, is all about putting ourselves in the driver's seat. It is scary because it is filled with unknown streets and curves and detours, but only then can we take credit for driving our own car into a destiny that is truly our own."

What Is Nick Doing Now?

Nick Lowery has set more records than can be counted, so what is he doing now? Nick is the host of one of the premier radio shows *HeadGames* on Sports Byline USA, SIRIUS Satellite Radio's Channel 122, and American Forces Network *(Headgamesradio.com)*. He is also the Acting Chair, National Fund for Excellence in American Indian Education. In 2004, Nick was a nominee for the NFL Hall of Fame. He is also one of the top motivational speakers on the circuit. In addition to all of Nick's work, he is still actively involved in many charities and charitable foundations.

Nick Lowery is an incredible man and has amassed an impressive body of work both on the field and off. He is an inspiration and an icon. If only we could all be a little bit more like Nick. To contact Nick, please email him at *email@headgamesradio.com* or visit either of his websites at *Nicklowery.com* and *HeadgamesRadio.com*.

Chapter 20
Football Definitions, Rules, Penalties and Fun Football Stats

A

Audible: An audible is a "play" initiated by the quarterback at the line of scrimmage. This play changes the one that was previously agreed upon in the huddle, thereby causing a change of plans prior to the ball going into play. An audible can also be called an automatic.

Automatic: See audible.

B

Balanced Line: A balanced line is a configuration with an equal number of linemen on either side of the center.

Birdcage: The facemask worn by linemen. The birdcage has extra vertical and horizontal bars across the front.

Blind Side: This refers to the opposite side a player on the team is looking towards.

Blitz: This is a concentrated run by linebackers and defensive backs. The linebackers and defensive backs charge through the offensive line in order to sack the quarterback before he can hand the ball off or before he is able to pass it. This maneuver is also known as "red dogging."

Bootleg: This move requires the quarterback to fake a hand-off to one of the backs then continue in the opposite direction to run or pass the ball.

Block: A block involves putting contact on an opponent with any part of the body. The basic block involves chest-to-chest contact. A shoulder block involves using the shoulder to contact. The scramble block is intended to tangle up an approaching challenger, who is playing another position. The scramble block is also known as a reach block. Finally, there is the pass block, which is used to delay the oncoming defensive line and allow your quarterback time to throw the ball.

Buttonhook: A buttonhook is a pass play where the receiver heads straight downfield, then unexpectedly turns back in the direction of the line of scrimmage.

C

Center: The center is an offensive line position at the center of the line of scrimmage. The center, as stated in chapter 7, snaps the ball to the quarterback or punter.

Chain Crew: The chain crew consists of three assistants to the officials. Their job entails handling the first-down measuring chain and the down box.

Cheap Shot: A cheap shot is just what it sounds like. It's a deliberate foul or other violent act against an unsuspecting player.

Check Off: This is the act of calling an audible.

Clipping: Clipping is to block an opponent from behind.

Clothesline: A clothesline involves hitting another player across the face with an extended arm.

Coffin Corner: This refers to any of the four corners of the field.

Coin Toss: This occurs before the start of the game. The quarterback of the visiting team calls heads or tails for a coin that is flipped by the referee. The winning team gets the kick off and the losing team gets to pick which goal to defend.

Completion: A completion is a legally caught pass.

Conversion: A conversion is a scoring play that occurs directly after a touchdown. This play involves either kicking the ball for one point or trying to add two bonus points by running or passing the ball into the end zone.

Cornerback: A defensive backfield player.

Cover: To guard a position or location on the field.

Crackback: A receiver who takes or moves to a position more than two yards outside the tackle.

Cut: When a player suddenly changes direction to lose a pursuing player. This is also what a coach and manager do to a player who is not meeting their expectations.

D

Dead Ball: A ball that is no longer in play due to an incomplete pass or a fumble.

Defense: The team defending their goal line.

Defensive Backfield: The area of the field or the players behind the defensive linemen.

Defensive Lineman: The defensive lineman rushes the quarterback in order to block progress or sack him.

Down: An offensive play that begins with a center snap and ends when the ball is dead.

Down and In: A tactic where the receiver runs straight downfield, then suddenly cuts in the direction of the middle of the field to throw off the opposing team.

Down and Out: A down and out is the direct opposite of a down and in play. The receiver runs downfield then turns out, in the direction of the sideline.

Draw Play: A fake pass that ends with one of the backs carrying the ball up the middle after the defensive linemen are "drawn in" on the pass rush.

E

Encroach: Having contact with an opposing team member before the snap.

End: An offensive lineman on the very end of the line of scrimmage.

End Line: There are two end lines and they are at the very end of the field on opposite sides.

End Zone: The area between the goal lines and the end lines, where the touchdown is made.

Extra Point: When a team scores a touchdown, they have the ability to earn one more point by making a successful place-kick.

F

Face Mask: The mask attached to the helmet and worn by the players.

Fair Catch: During the punt, a receiver designated to catch the ball signals to his team that he will not advance after catching it.

False Start: When an offensive player moves before the ball is snapped.

Field Goal: When a place-kick goes through the goalpost, worth three points.

Flanker: An offensive player on the right or left side of the configuration.

Flood: An attempt to inundate the opposition in a particular area of the field with a formidable amount of players.

Forward Pass: Throwing the ball towards the opponents' goal.

Foul: Breaking of the rules.

Freeze: Holding onto the ball for a long period of time without scoring or attempting to score.

Front Four: The teams' defensive front line, which consists of two ends and two tackles.

Fullback: The player whose job it is to block for the halfback and quarterback.

Fumble: When a ball is dropped while in play.

G

Goal Line: The line that the ball must pass over in order to score a touchdown.

Goal Line Stand: When the opposing team attempts to block a touchdown by standing near the goal line.

Guard: An offensive lineman.

H

Hail Mary: A Hail Mary is when the quarterback throws the ball in the air without targeting a particular receiver.

Hang Time: The length of time a punt remains in the air.

Halfback: A halfback's job is to run the ball, block, and receive passes. They are also known as a running back or tailback.

Handoff: When one teammate hands the ball off to another.

Hash Marks: Divides the field into thirds.

Hitch and Go: When a runner goes downfield to catch a pass but fakes a quick turn instead.

Holder: The player who holds the ball during a place kick.

Holding: An illegal use of hands or an illegal block above the waist in an attempt to keep another player from advancing down the field.

Huddle: The offensive players get in a group to set up the next play.

I

Illegal Low Block: Blocking another player below the knees.

Illegal Motion: An illegal movement by an offensive player prior to the snap.

Illegal Procedure: A penalty that includes movement by an offensive player before the snap.

Incomplete: A forward pass that is not caught by the receiver.

Intentional Grounding: When the quarterback intentionally throws the ball out of bounds or into the ground to avoid throwing a pass that he thinks may be intercepted.

Interception: An interception is a pass that is caught by a defensive player, giving his team possession of the ball.

Interference: Illegally blocking a player's chance to catch a pass.

K

Key: Watching the opposing team's members for subtle movements in order to see what they are going to do.

Kick: Kicking the ball in order to score additional points after a touchdown or score points on a field goal.

Kickoff: Kicking the ball to begin the game.

L

Lateral: A lateral is a sideways or backwards pass thrown from one player to another.

Linebacker: A linebacker's job is to tackle runners and block or intercept passes.

Line Judge: An official who watches for various violations and illegal procedures.

Lineman: The players on the forward line.

Line of Scrimmage: An imaginary line used to determine where the players will line up.

Live Ball: A ball that is in play.

M

Man in Motion: This is the player who turns and runs behind the line of scrimmage or parallel to it during the call of the signals. Once the ball is snapped by the center, he then proceeds downfield.

Man-to-man Defense: This is where each team member covers someone on the offense.

Middle Guard: A middle guard is the defensive lineman who is positioned between the tackles directly opposite the offensive center.

Multiple Offenses: This is a strategy used by the offense and combining a number of different formations.

N

Nickel Defense: A nickel defense is the defensive configuration that requires five defensive backs.

Numbering System: This is the system the NFL uses to identify the positions of the players. It works as follows:
    1-19: Quarterbacks and kickers.
    20-49: Defensive and running backs.
    50-59: Linebackers and centers.
    60-79: Defensive linemen and offensive linemen.
    80-89: Wide receivers and tight ends.

O

Offense: The team that currently has the football.

Offensive Backfield: The area or players that are behind the offensive linemen.

Offensive Linemen: The offensive linemen are the seven players that include the center, two guards, two ends and two tackles.

Official: The person who interprets the rules of the game.

Offside: Offside occurs when a player on one of the teams is over the opposing team's line of scrimmage before the ball is snapped by the center.

Onside Kick: A short kick that usually moves just beyond 10 yards.

Open Up Holes: This allows a team to move forward through the defense by blocking and opening up holes amongst the defenders.

Option Play: An option play is an offensive play where the player who holds the football has the choice of running or passing the ball.

Outside: The area towards the sideline.

Overtime: Overtime occurs when a tie needs to be broken. In professional football, the first team to score a touchdown wins the overtime. This is also called "sudden death."

P

Pass Pattern: The precise course a receiver runs in order to catch a pass.

Pass Rush: The "rush" by the defense to tackle or pressure the quarterback before he can complete a pass.

Penalty: A penalty is castigation due to a foul or other illegal procedure.

Piling On: This occurs when a number of players jump on the player with the ball after he's been tackled.

Place Kick: A place kick is a kick made when the ball is held in place on the ground.

Play Action Pass: This occurs when the quarterback fakes a handoff to a running back while he's moving back to set himself up to make the real pass.

Playbook: The notebook that contains a team's terms, strategies, plans, plays, etc. and is issued to each player on the team.

Playmaker: This term is generally used for the person on the team who is considered "skilled" at helping their team score points.

Pocket: The spot from which the quarterback sets up his pass.

Point After Touchdown: After a touchdown, a team may score an additional point with a successful place kick through the opposition's goal post.

Post Pattern: A prearranged course run by a receiver in an effort to become open for a pass.

Power Sweep: A running play where two or more offensive linemen pull out of their stances and run toward the outside of the line of scrimmage.

Primary Receiver: The receiver chosen by the quarterback in the huddle to receive the ball.

Pulling: This occurs when a player leaves his position to move to another place on the field in order to block.

Pump Fake: This happens when the quarterback pulls his arm back to fake a forward pass.

Punt: A kicker takes the football, drops it from his hands and then kicks it before it hits the ground.

Punt Return: A punt return occurs when the ball is received and run back by the opposing team towards the punting team's side.

Q

Quarter: There are four quarters to every football game. Each quarter is 15 minutes long.

Quarterback: The offensive player who receives the ball from the center during the snap.

Quarterback Sneak: This occurs when the quarterback receives the ball after the snap and instantly runs forward through the opposition lines.

Quick Count: These are the calls that the quarterback makes rapidly at the line of scrimmage.

Quick Kick: A quick kick is a surprise punt.

R

Ready List: A ready list is a short list of plays specifically customized for a future game.

Receiver: A receiver's job is to get into the open on the field and catch a pass from the quarterback.

Recovery: This occurs when a team member grabs a ball that has been fumbled.

Red Dog: A red dog is a defensive plan in which a linebacker or defensive back abandons his usual task in order to force the quarterback to change his play.

Returner: A team member who runs back kickoffs and punts.

Reverse: A reverse happens when the running back receives a handoff from the quarterback, continues laterally behind the line of scrimmage then hands the ball off to a receiver running in the reverse direction.

Roll: A roll occurs when the quarterback moves right or left with the ball before passing it.

Roster: A list of team members.

Roughing: This is any personal foul where one player comes into contact with another player outside of the accepted boundaries of the game.

Running Back: A running back is the position behind the quarterback.

Rush: A rush means to run from the scrimmage line with the football.

S

Sack: When a quarterback is tackled before he can throw a pass.

Safety: A safety has two meanings in football. One is a two-point score by the defense and the other is a defensive backfield player who generally plays deeper than the cornerbacks.

Safety Blitz: A defensive maneuver where one or both safeties attempt to sack the quarterback.

Safety Valve: A safety valve is a short pass that is thrown to a running back when the quarterback can't find an open receiver to throw the ball to before the pass rush closes in.

Scramble: A scramble occurs when the quarterback runs behind the line of scrimmage to avoid being sacked.

Scrambler: A scrambler is a quarterback who has a reputation for scrambling.

Screen Pass: A screen pass is a pass from behind the line of scrimmage by the quarterback.

Scrimmage: The battle along the line amongst two teams, beginning when the football is snapped by the center.

Secondary: The secondary is the defensive backfield or second line of defense.

Shift: The movement of two offensive players between positions.

Signals: The information that the quarterback gives to the other players regarding what the next play will be.

Slant: A slant occurs when the ball is run at an angle.

Slot: The gap in the offensive line between a receiver and a tackle.

Snap: The handing off of the ball by the center to the quarterback or punter.

Spearing: Illegal contact using the player's head.

Special Teams: A special group of players that concentrate on one particular tactic or strategy in the game.

Spiral: The way a football rotates when it's thrown.

Split End: A split end is a receiver who lines up several yards away from the next player alongside the line of scrimmage.

Square In - Out: A pass pattern where the runner goes downfield then turns "in" at a "square" or "out" to the sideline.

Squib Kick: A squib kick is a low, flat kickoff.

Stunt: An abnormal charge by the offensive linemen.

Substitution: When the coach substitutes one player for another

T

Tackle: To bring the player carrying the ball down to the field and ending the play.

Tailback: A member of the offensive backfield.

T - Formation: An offensive configuration with three running backs in the backfield.

Three-point Stance: The stance that players form at the line of scrimmage prior to the snap

Tight End: An offensive player who serves as a receiver as well as a blocker.

Touchback: A play where the kicked football is ruled to be dead on or behind a team's own goal line.

Touchdown: When a player carries into or catches the ball in the other team's end zone and receives six points.

Trap Block: A trap block occurs when the opposing team allows a member of the other team to proceed through the "enemy line." At that time, the opposing team blocks him by surprise.

Turnover: When one team loses the ball to the opposing team by fumble or interception.

U

Unbalanced Line: A formation with more players on one side of the center than the other.

Uprights: The uprights are the vertical posts on either end of the goalposts.

V

Veer: A quick-hitting run when the ball is given to a running back.

W

Wishbone Formation: An offensive formation that includes one fullback and two halfbacks positioned in the backfield.

Wide Out: An offensive player who positions himself on or near the line of scrimmage.

Wide Receiver: A wide receiver is the same as a wide out.

Wild Card: The two playoff berths awarded in each conference to the two non-division winning teams that have the top records in the conference.

X

X's and O's: The diagrams used for the game plays.

Y

Yardage: The amount of yards lost or gained during a play.

Z

Zone Defense: A defense plan whereby each player is assigned to a "zone" on the field that they are required to defend.

Penalties
Illegal procedures that incur five yard penalties:

Delay of game
Defensive holding or illegal use of hands
Encroachment
Excessive time outs
False Start
Forward pass thrown from behind the line of scrimmage after the
    ball has already crossed the line
Forward pass thrown from beyond the line of scrimmage
Illegal formation
Illegal shift
Illegal motion
Illegal substitution
Invalid fair catch signal
Illegal return
Too many men on the field
Offside
Pass touched by a receiver after being out of bounds
Player out of bounds at snap
Running into the kicker
Second forward pass behind the line
Unintentional facemask

Illegal procedures that incur ten yard penalties:

Deliberately batting, kicking, or punching a loose ball
Helping the runner
Holding, illegal use of hands, illegal block above the waist
Intentional grounding
Offensive pass interference
Tripping

Illegal procedures that incur fifteen yard penalties:

Chop block
Clipping
Facemask
Fair catch interference
Faking a roughing
Illegal low block
Kicking or kneeling on an opponent
Roughing the kicker
Roughing the passer
Spearing
Striking an official
Striking an opponent with a fist
Unnecessary roughness
Unsportsmanlike conduct
Using a helmet as a weapon

CHAPTER 21
Epilogue

When the title for this book first popped into my head a few summers ago, I thought, "Sure...yeah...right! How in the world can I write a book on this subject? I'm a woman! I can communicate my needs and feelings-- but to write a book on women and relate some of that subject matter to football? That's crazy!" While I have written other books, this one definitely seemed out of my league.

Even so, I did put the title down in my computer and stored it there. Just in case. I told God that if He wanted me to write it, He would have to put the words on the page for me. And despite all of my best efforts to block the book from my head over the next five months, it continued to plague my mind like those nagging, insignificant errands that I never really want to take the time to do. Finally, I remembered *Proverbs 16:9:* "In his heart a man plans his course, but the Lord determines his steps." And I knew from experience, that if I sat down and did the "errand," the weight would come off of my shoulders.

And yet, I couldn't do it. I was trying but I was forgetting about *Mark 10:27,* where the Bible clearly states that, "All things are possible with God." For months, I was constantly talking to my family and friends about the concept of the book and its title. I also continued to pray, "God, if you want me to write this book, you will have to write it for me. I am absolutely incapable of writing such a book."

Matthew 14:28 - 31 gives us a perfect picture of how God can take us out of our comfort zone and bring us to him. In this story, Simon Peter was sitting comfortably and safely in a boat, when Jesus suddenly asked him to walk on the water together. The story continues, *"...and Peter answered him, 'Lord, if it is you, bid me come to you on the water.'"* When the Lord did so, Peter got out of the boat and walked on the water, coming toward Jesus. When he saw the wind, though, he was afraid, letting his confidence give way and his feet begin to sink. Desperately, *"he cried out, 'Lord, save me.' Jesus immediately reached out his hand and caught him saying to him, 'O man of little faith, why did you doubt?'"*

In this story, Peter was definitely out of his comfort zone, yet Jesus brought him safely across the water. Thinking about this, my mind wondered, "Why couldn't I be more like Peter?" Still, doubt in my own abilities persisted and I continued to put off writing the book, ignoring God's word that He works best in those who lack ability. I continued to struggle, praying, "God, please help!"

Well, eventually God did come to my rescue. One night in December, dreaming about the entire first chapter, I took the hint and started to write, completing the first 30 pages very quickly. Then, I stopped. By mid-January, I had let life interfere with God's plan for me, so wrapped up in what was happening around me that I had completely given up on the book. I had again lost confidence and decided that the book was too daunting a task for me to undertake.

Over the next several months, life became very complicated. The more I tried to patch up, bandage and solve all the problems surrounding me, the worse they became. I finally made the decision to give everything over to the Lord, getting back to the book and praying for Him to fill the in gaps made by my inadequacies.

Once I had done all of this, a true peace finally came over me. Everywhere I turned, thoughts poured into my head and the words then flew onto my computer. Whether I was in my car, the shower or even the middle of a movie, I couldn't stop the flow. Sometimes, it was really quite comical to be in the shower and suddenly finding myself looking for a piece of paper!

So, this book is dedicated to God for taking all of the distractions in my life away for a season, forcing me to go beyond my comfort zone and into one marked by inadequacy, where He works best. Thank you, Lord! I feel myself shouting out the words of *Corinthians 12:9-10*, *"...but He said to me, My grace is sufficient for you, for my power is made perfect in weakness. I will all the more gladly boast of my weaknesses, that the power of Christ may rest upon me.'"*

This book is also dedicated to my Mom. Without her loving kindness, support, faith and patience during this past year full of all my personal trials, I would not have made it through. Thank you, Mom. You have done so much for me. Thank you for giving me the gift of sight. It has really changed my life.

Also, a special thank you goes out to Mark for fixing my 'puter and to my sister, Jeri, for teaching me some new tricks in formatting. A big thank you to Albert for his creative skills and for making this book come to life!

A huge thank you goes to the sweetest man on this Earth, Bruce. Thank you my dear and precious man for all that you have given, thank you for your creative inspiration and thank you for all the help you have offered to make me keep pushing this project forward. All my love...Jaci Rae - *"The Rae of HopeTM"*

Bibliography

i AlleyDog.com Psychology Glossary

iii, v, vi, vii, viii From The American Heritage Dictionary.

ix Data used from the Center for Non-Verbal Studies.

x, xi, xii, xiii, xiv, xv, xvi, xvii, xviii, xix, xx From The American Heritage Dictionary.

xxi Data used from the Center For Non-Verbal Studies.

xxii, xxiii, xxiv, xxv From The American Heritage Dictionary.

xxvi, xxvii, xxviii, xxix, xxx http://www.healthwell.com/delicious-online/d_backs/Jul_02/update.cfm?path=hw and http://www.oxytocin.org/

Note:

All Biblical References have been taken from the New American Standard Bible and The Kings James Bible.

All Fun Football Facts, rules of engagement, football statistics and other football historical facts have been taken from the following sites (all football facts are current as of 2005):
http://www..NFL.com
http://www.football.com/rulesandinfo.shtml
http://www.profootballhof.com/

Additional Football History taken from:
http://www.4worldrecords.4anything.com

ABOUT THE AUTHOR

Jaci Rae: Singer, Writer...Renaissance Woman

She could have just been a singing star and that would have been enough.

It would have been enough - more than enough - for anyone with a fabulous voice and a dream. Win the GMA's *"Female Vocalist of the Year"* . . . earn the prestigious Levi Strauss award . . . garner a bunch of other industry awards...release some fantastic CDs as Jaci has √ and the average person could have died then with a great, big smile on their face.

Jaci Rae is not your average person.

Far from it, in fact. She is that rare woman in command of a range of creative skills, thoroughly able to impact the world with each one.

A Singer...Like a River

When Jaci started out in the music business, she was the greenest of greenies. An outsider's outsider. Faced with those kinds of impossible odds, the hopes of hundreds of thousands of other would-be singing stars have withered on the vine and died.

It only made Jaci all the more determined.

She had little idea how to launch her own singing career. There were, after all, no manuals on the subject available to a poor child. So she learned. Several years of trial and error later - of learning what made music execs and their unusual industry tick - yielded success. Great success in fact. To date, Jaci has achieved four number one singles in her brand of heartfelt country...plus a number one spot on the CMA charts in Europe.

Her latest CD, *Can't Push a River*, is a critical and commercial success. Said DJ, Chris Allen, from *Big Kat 98.9* in Minnesota : "There is so much heart and soul in Jaci's music! Incredible CD!" More praise followed. "This is a great CD. The first 2 songs are especially Terrific. All in all it's a great CD and should do well for her," said Grand Ole Opry Star, Ernie Ashworth.

And from across the pond, Raymond Phillips from *Country Harvest Radio* in Australia said, "*Can't Push a River* is truly a first class product, something Jaci can really be proud of from the first to the last track!" And the list goes on!

Accomplish this much and people will call you a leader. But Jaci was just getting started.

Cutting a Path to Music Success

... Then Mapping the Way

Not everyone can write. Fortunately, Jaci Rae can.
With that talent, she has given others the roadmap to music success she never had.

It's called *The Ultimate Guide to Music Success*. To many budding singing stars, it is the single missing piece in their music career puzzle.

"WOW! Jaci Rae's book, *The Ultimate Guide To Music Success*, is what I have been looking for all along!" said singer, Justin Timestin. He's not alone. With the Guide's help, Reginald Owens and his partner, "not only got college bookings, radio, and Internet airplay, but also the number nine spot in the *CMJ* (College Music Journal)."

The thing is, testimonials like these are typical of the feedback Jaci's book generates. *The Ultimate Guide to Music Success* has changed (and will change) the destinies of struggling singers and musicians throughout America .

But here's what's so remarkable: Not everyone returns after they've achieved success to help others succeed, too .

Jaci is that rare person.

Writing Relationship Wrongs

Helping relationships succeed is another of Jaci's crusades.

The fact that so many marriages crash and burn is an issue with her. To Jaci, it's just common sense that good relationships boil down to good communication . That was an important lesson Jaci learned early on as a counselor for troubled youth.

With all their science, psychologists and psychiatrists still don't have the answer to the divorce epidemic (collectively, the group has an outrageous divorce rate of 90 percent). Jaci knew that and struggled to come up with her own model for teaching, her own style for instructing principles of communication in relationships.

She found it in football, of all places.

Winning Points with the Woman in Your Life ™ is an original work, a refreshing, slightly tongue-in-cheek comparison of football and relationships that gives men a memorable way of visualizing male/female action and reaction.

"The award-winning singer's 10th book tackles the subject of improving romantic relation-ships. Cleverly using football plays, scrimmage strategies, and tactical maneuvers as analo-gies, she shows the male reader how to score big points with their woman," wrote Richard Leiby of *The Washington Post*.

Couples have already written to thank her for the huge help this book has been. But this is just one more impact from a very impactful woman.

Renaissance Lady

With her tenth self-help book completed, with her music career firmly on course, with all of these accomplishments coming at a very early age, Jaci remains grateful for her blessings and excited about the future.

Her future will undoubtedly include many new achievements.

A "Renaissance Woman" is someone accomplished in a number of fields, including the arts and sciences.

What a perfect way to describe Jaci Rae.

For more on Jaci, go to: www.jacirae.com

CATALOGUE

If you enjoyed this book, you will enjoy Jaci Rae's other books and products.

Jaci Rae's Latest and best CD: *Can't Push A River* $12.98

To find more on Jaci Rae's books and products, or to listen to sound bites from her CDs, go to: http://www.jacirae.com

Here are a few reviews from around the world on Jaci's latest CD:

"This is a great CD. The first 2 songs are Terrific. All in all it's a great CD and it should do well for her." *Ernie Ashworth, Grand Ole Opry Star*

"Jaci Rae does her finest work to date...these are the songs that formed her, no wonder why there is so much heart and soul in them." *Chris Allen, Big Kat 98.9*

"Can't Push a River" is truly a first class product, something Jaci can really be proud of from the first to the last track. It has made my task hard to choose which one should be used first for airplay. Definitely marked for regular rotation on Country Harvest. CONGRATULATIONS on "Can't Push a River" *Raymond Phillips, Country Harvest Radio, Australia*

"Jaci Rae's combination of musical prowess, passionate vocals and high-energy stage presence make Jaci Rae an artist to watch." *Rob Simbeck, ABC Radio Networks*

To order any of Jaci's products, send a cashiers check or money order, or include your M/C or Visa number with expiration date, address, and phone number and mail to:

North Shore Records
P. O. Box 1118, Felton, CA 95018
info@jacirae.com

For more convenience and faster turn - around, please go to our website and order these products using our secure server: http://www.jacirae.com

(CA residents please include 8.25% tax)
(Do not include shipping price when calculating taxes. For all overseas and other Int'l orders, please email your location and we will calculate the shipping costs and send them to you via email.)

Printed in the United States
by Baker & Taylor Publisher Services